Sustaining The League of Women Voters in America

Sustaining The League of Women Voters in America

Maria Hoyt Cashin

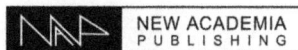

NEW ACADEMIA
PUBLISHING

Washington, DC

New Academia Publishing 2013

Library of Congress Control Number: 2013930330
ISBN 978-0-9860216-9-5 paperback (alk. paper)

New Academia Publishing
PO Box 27420, Washington, DC 20038-7420
info@newacademia.com - www.newacademia.com

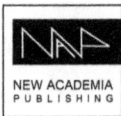

This manuscript also exists in slightly different thesis form under the title: "The Democratic Merit and Sustainability of Participatory Public Interest Associations: A Case Study of the League of Women Voters."

Contents

Preface

Democratic associations are cause for both hope and concern in contemporary America. Many well-known groups that inspired active, bridging membership to expand representation have disbanded or shrunk because of shifting social and political culture. In their place, the bulk of current associations are rigid hierarchies that cement difference in practice and operate without viable membership direction or participation. In structural, purposive and developmental contrast to that trend, the League of Women Voters is frequently cited as a laudable civic enterprise that models a positive democratic association. Critics do exist, charging for example that by virtue of its association form, the League is simply another interest group and thus subject to scrutiny for self-serving purpose, fallible focus and manipulated process. But close examination will support an argument that the League is unusually capable of rendering internal and external democratic benefits through its enhancement of personalized and national democratic process, reliance on consensus and deliberation, and systematic pursuit of a public interest.

In order to better understand what makes an association democratically beneficial, this book takes an interdisciplinary approach. It considers the League of Women Voters' origins, evolution, record, membership, and gradually declining numbers in the context of democratic theory, American history, and organizational study. These combined perspectives pose reasons for the League's longevity and enable a forecast, through its prospects, for the character of future self-rule through civic-focused associations. The fact that the League faces uncertain future while other sectarian, hierarchical and, in some cases, democracy-disabling groups are thriving is due at least in part to a deep public divide on whether citizen participation is a positive element in contemporary American democracy. Yet democracy can only be valid in theory and legitimate in practice if more people exhibit appreciation for their citizenship and its constitutionally set terms. To strengthen engaged self-rule that draws from public interest groups like the League, Americans need to reinvigorate a national civic culture that regulates and expands fair participation, tolerates and benefits from difference, and looks forward through deliberative process toward an enlarged public interest that breeds both legitimate citizen assent and responsible policy and governance. That form of legitimacy amounts to a definition of the League's history and promise, underlining a judgment that it should be protected from some form of Camelot-like fate through closer appreciation of its contributions to democracy.

Acknowledgments

The fact that this book has moved forward is testimony to the terrific support of Thomas M. Kerch, PhD during the closing year of my recent graduate studies at Georgetown University. He provided wise council on democratic theory, conducted careful analysis of my argument and gamely took on exploration of the Progressive Era, women's suffrage and the League of Women Voters. I also extend deep gratitude to my husband Steve and children Oliver, Madeleine and Ben for encouraging me through extended months of research and writing. Rachel Shone kindly obtained membership data from the Daughters of the American Revolution and set up the graphs in Appendices 1 and 2. Charles Yonkers, JD and Emily Hoechst, PhD provided invaluable advice for clarifying my message as it shifted to book form. Finally and most importantly, members and staff of the League of Women Voters graciously welcomed engagement and discussion for which I am extremely appreciative; the resulting participation in social gatherings, annual meetings and private audiences was invaluable for fathoming the character and makeup of their justly celebrated deliberative operation.

Part I

National Trends

1

Introduction:

Do We Care About Personal Democracy?

American democratic institutions are built upon a guarded faith in a limited but developmental capacity of the country's citizens to actualize freedom, equality and self-determination through the exercise of their democratic rights. If indeed this exercise has atrophied with misuse, as pre-2008 voting records and November 2010 election returns suggest, the question is whether the loss of freedom, equality and self-determination via those institutions can be far behind. The exercise of democratic rights is theoretically a deliberate activity, to be activated or bypassed by individual choice. But in practice, obstructions abound to deter participation. Citizen engagement in process is deeply affected by available vehicles to link both passive and proactive citizens with the quality of their governmental representation and their perception of its legitimacy.

An alternative vernacular title to this work could be *America! Eat Your Own Home-Grown Spinach Before Presenting it for Someone Else's Consumption*. Active citizenship is personally compelling to me, in part because of the many years I've lived and traveled in Africa. In the midst of extended residence in Nairobi, Kenya during the 1980s and 1990s, I witnessed incredible bravery on a widespread scale, as people struggled for expression, solidarity, decent living standards and tolerant self-rule during the height of that country's democracy movement. For the last seven years, I've been intimately connected with Liberia, as its people struggle to take a democratic path away from a violent past. In both cases, those citizens are very aware of two realities Americans seem to forget: To protect citizen rights and accompanying benefits, people need to energize, educate themselves and vote. Institutional democratic process is a gift to that end, provided participation is full and fair. Returning from sundry places like Kenya and Liberia, I am dumbfounded to find Americans assertively disengaged from both their internationally touted democratic process and the shared aspects of their civil society. They remain unconvinced of their obligation to exercise their rights, so hard won by past generations. I'm not alone in this concern. Increasing numbers of scholars are convinced that reforming American democracy at home is far more pressing than experimenting in self-congratulating democracy promotion abroad. The first step should be nonpartisan dedication to revitalizing a national civic culture to get the country back on track.

Present levels of disengagement and resulting disenchantment are not intrinsic to the United States. Participatory associations have historically and theoretically been judged tremendously important to America's civic character, for they appear to have encouraged, enabled and enlarged a widespread, repeated engagement that has contributed on a personal and societal level to achieving Alexis de Tocqueville's celebrated "self-interest properly understood." Tocqueville had suggested in the first half of the 19th century that Americans' tendency to band together in association expanded their sense of self-interest and guarded against their individualistic tendencies to retreat into cocooned personal worlds.[1] Although the level of this "banding" and evidence of its positive effects have fluctuated throughout the nation's history, our society's affiliating proclivity has become integral to national self-image for contrasting reasons. Associations are seen variously as brakes to government growth through preserving private potential, social reengagement recipes for frustrated citizenry, expertise augmenters that enable informed participation, or allied builders of a common interest in the public sphere. Increasingly, they are also considered to be propaganda vehicles with cloudy legislative agendas. Because of this range in interpretation and practice, political theorist Mark E. Warren cautions in *Democracy and Associations* that Americans should carefully consider associations' character and effect before embracing their personal or societal appeal. He notes that there has been little work on "*what* we should expect associations to do for democracies or *why* we should expect associations to carry out these democratic functions."[2]

In that spirit, I have set out to examine how civic associations operate in practice and to assess their chances for survival in the unregulated nonprofit climate established by the Supreme Court's 2010 decision regarding Citizens United versus the Federal Election Commission. There are considerable democratic stakes in their fortunes. The League of Women Voters (henceforth frequently termed the League) presents a compelling choice for a case study since it is literally dedicated to strengthening and expanding democracy. But its example also contains complexity and a degree of uneven performance. Like any human endeavor, the League's makeup and operation will pull it in several different directions to varying applause. Some critics might charge that by virtue of its association form, it is simply another interest group seeking the success of its own self-serving, if public-spirited agenda. Admirers, however, will claim that its process and achievements should be emulated and preserved.

This book takes an interdisciplinary approach to explore what makes one association democratically beneficial and consider whether such findings matter on a larger scale. It considers the League of Women Voters' origins, evolution, record, membership, and gradually declining numbers in the context of democratic theory, American history, and organizational study. These combined perspectives help pose reasons for the League's longevity and enable a forecast, through its prospects, for the character of future self-rule through civic-focused associations.

The League of Women Voters is an association that can be said to provide "democratic effects" through its operations linking individual citizens with the public sphere. In fact, it could be argued that the organization provides the "social substance of liberal-democratic procedures."[3] As such, it provides a dramatic departure from the professionalized and closeted association models of our time. Over the course of its ninety-two year nonpartisan history, the League has committed itself to the motivation, enablement and education of both its uniquely engaged members and those of the nation at-large on active citizenship, contemporary issues, and advocacy to promote reformed democratic process and equitable participation. Answering Warren's challenge to examine the impact and rationale for associations' engagement with democracy, this book will argue that the compelling component is the League's "why." (The essence of association motivation to engage in civics is, of course, highly telling for impact in developing democracies like Kenya and Liberia as well.) Direct descendants of the seventy-two year suffragist battle to win votes for women, the League's Progressive founders pledged to make that fight worthwhile by launching the League to help women *and* men vote freely, regularly and wisely to improve their country while passing on a legacy of cherished, hard-won and activated citizenship. This motivation to equip newly empowered female voters helped insure its dedication to internal self-governance and developmental substantive operation. Examination of the League will illustrate how, if one judges Warren's equation four paragraphs back to be important to democracy, it is particularly critical to consider *how* associations judged democratically beneficial act in practice in order to advance national social capital through their operation. The League passes the democratic bar most fundamentally by making self-rule in America's great geographical, demographic and technological span achievable on a practical daily level.

Rating the League on an association scale is a distinctly relative task. Judging by public relations campaigns and political activity in 2012, associations continue to actively promote interest and invite partisan combination. For reasons made clear within Chapters 2 and 3, most of the financially thriving groups will be found decidedly lacking in democratic potential regardless of message, membership numbers or facebook "likes." Social capital theorist Robert D. Putnam concluded the Twentieth Century with presentation of worrisome membership trends in associations and the accompanying decline in civic engagement and social capital. He made an important clarification about associations that are high in numbers yet operate essentially as "'tertiary' organizations . . . in which 'membership is essentially an honorific rhetorical device for fundraising.'"[4] Examples of these numerous groups include the National

Rifle Association and the American Civil Liberties Union, both of which rank within the top ten associations in terms of contributing members but also provide minimal opportunity for individual engagement. It is these national trends toward mysterious, elite direction of groups that shape public opinion and command large resources which make consideration of the League of Women Voters' democratic potential particularly significant. As professionalism grows in the previously volunteer-driven association world, well-financed extremist voices influence the public agenda, and the diversity of American people retreats voluntarily or through compulsion from civic life. As evidence of the latter, some previously flourishing local chapters of the League are disbanding, and its leadership is pondering how to compete and retain character. The League's future may be of interest far beyond its membership, as prospects for deliberative self-rule decline.

Material for the case study is rich but, until now, nonintegrated. Different labels could apply to the League, and each has its own literature. Given its central role in activating the Nineteenth Amendment, some researchers examine it as a feminist organization dedicated to expanding the rights of women. Historians also examine its link with the character and intent of the original Progressives. Deliberative democrats focus on its encouragement of public dialogue about contentious issues. Public administrators study its record in propelling the identification and encouragement of collective action to deal with wide-impact problems in a public interest fashion. Those compelled by Putnam's lament on a decline of bridging interaction will celebrate its active and theoretically diverse membership. Voting practitioners will focus on its provision of nonpartisan materials, events and advocacy that strengthen Americans' ability to vote on election days. Some political scientists consider its operation as an interest group, pairing its effectiveness on "public" agendas with the personal interests of its supporters.

Interesting as some of the alternative angles may be, my primary focus is to address Warren's measure of a democratically beneficial association. Perhaps unsurprisingly, my conclusion is that the League of Women Voters fits Warren's socio-cultural definition of a civically virtuous, democracy-promoting association with a "distinct disposition that underwrite[s] democratic process, including a willingness to play by the rules, attend to the common good, trust others, empathize with others, tolerate differences, respect rights, and deliberate and listen in good faith."[5]

But theoretical approbation doesn't sustain day-to-day operation. Given the besieged character of such an association and the concurrent imperative to reenergize an ailing national civic culture, I will argue that there is considerable reason to publicly sustain civic groups like the League of Women Voters. Such intervention could be either indirect or targeted and still have consequence. Prioritizing national civic education would likely draw from the League's legacy and re-inspire its future. Public valuing of citizenship would alter individual motivation to join. Reforming the nonprofit sector and clarifying the definition of a civic membership group would make personal choices clearer and enable tax policy adjustment for the sector. Experimenting in public rewards or penalties for civic actions might increase free time for public duties and energize those previously disinclined. Policing fair association practice could help avoid bullying from other wealthy partisan groups intent on specific outcome.

To head toward that conclusion, the book contains three sections. Part I on National Trends includes this Introduction as Chapter 1. Chapter 2 examines the highly diverse theory affecting American associations, attempts an association typology and explores their diverse relationships with the public, government and democratic practice over time. Chapter 3 ponders what affects associations' democratic merits on individual, cultural and self-governing grounds, reviewing arguments in favor of public interest orientation and active membership. Chapter 4 considers research on civic association member characteristics, motivations and trends. Chapter 5 examines dwindling memberships and considers general tools and viruses that affect association sustainability.

With those national trends in place, Part II on The League's Promise begins to explore why the League of Women Voters is such a compelling contemporary case study for the relationship between American democracy and associations. Chapter 6 considers the League in historical context, looking at how its Suffrage origins and early struggles impacted its structural and purposive evolution. It further gauges its distinctive style and function, the consistent dedication to grassroots process, and particular characteristics of its membership. Chapter 7 applies the earlier-described standards of democratically beneficial public interest associations to the League. At a general level, its record will be determined by activity within its mission areas: fostering education on citizenship, preparing and energizing people for democratic engagement, and encouraging the formation of "enlarged" public opinion. But the reality will prove a bit more complicated. Thus, the chapter considers whether the League's progressive advocacy compromises nonpartisanship or public interest representation and whether public problems do get solved in an enlarged fashion through its efforts. Attention will be devoted to its dedication to respecting the democratic process, its contributions toward social trust, and its identification and pursuit of the common good. Limitations flowing from difference and positions on gender advocacy will be considered. Tensions will be explored between institutional preservation and social impact. Finally, I will explore the degree of institutional compensation for democratic effects rendered.

The Argument for Sustaining Particular Democratic Associations contained within the Conclusion in Part Three, Chapter 8 will focus on the national stakes in survival of civic membership groups. It questions whether public interest membership groups like the League of Women Voters remain important and viable within contemporary America. Do they contribute toward shared values, and what are the stakes if particular ones disband? As particularized advocacy takes off without financial constraints, the voice of "public interest" is becoming faint and less effective, leading some to disagree that public participation, as sometimes "contracted out" through associations, is beneficial to democratic culture. Trends toward heightened partisanship and disengaged citizenry may demonstrate serious implications for national democratic legitimacy, and suggest self-rule is dangerously off-track and vulnerable to hijacking. Yet close examination hints that solutions may reside in the very degree of the approaching debacle.

2

Legend and History:

Democracy and Civic Membership Associations in America

While the League of Women Voters is one of the most frequently analyzed American associations, its examination tends to break into narrow archival form. But considering it more generally within the contexts of political theory and American history as they relate particularly to civic associations unveils both a deeper understanding of the League and our country's challenges in overcoming contradictions between ideal democracy and its practical application. The League will provide a provocative test case for these tensions within Chapters 6 and 7, given its civic origins, enduring purpose and ninety-two years of practice in helping Americans engage, through associations, in informed self-governance.

Mark E. Warren describes a wide American consensus that "the virtues and viability of a democracy depend on the robustness of its associational life."[1] By tradition, such operation is purported to widen the experience of democracy beyond the voting booth into daily life, strengthening civic capacity in the process. Yet such belief rests on incomplete and conflicting theory. To clarify associations' reputed and actual importance, Warren has advocated a theoretical focus on what society expects associations to contribute toward healthy democracy as well as an examination of their motivation to do so. He has further urged consideration of *how* associations should operate so as to breed "democratic associational ecologies" that generate democratic effects.[2]

While the U.S. Constitution is silent beyond Amendment I's instruction that Congress "make no law… abridging the freedom of speech… or the right of people peaceably to assemble," Americans have consistently linked associations with their experience of democracy. At the same time, they have disagreed on associations' merits and confused their terminology. Grant Jordan and William A. Maloney observe, "the unquestioning acceptance of the (newly fashionable) term 'civil society' conjoined with the new intellectual associations of the term, has lead to a positive bestowal of legitimacy on what were once seen as interest groups. The democratic credentials of associations in the interest group guise were seen as deficient. However, a group in civil society robes appears more (normatively) wholesome and attractive."[3] However termed, the interest group argument, wherein associations "excel at capturing the *intensity of interest* of a fragmented public"[4] to help keep government accountable and the citizenry alert, reveals only one side of association potential. As examination of the League of Women Voters will make clear, the literal act of association has a developmental impact far beyond the interests promoted.

Past arguments that associations can exist as a sector divorced from public concerns and government operation have receded in recognition of the highly interdependent relationships across civil society in the Twenty-first Century. As these complex connections have developed, so too has the diversity within associations themselves. Some have members and serve particular interests; others have none, and seek public cause. Most are nonprofits in their financial structure, yet some compensate lucratively and pursue financial gain. Some are thriving; others are struggling or have already shrunk beyond return. Supposedly independent, the combined independent sector is riddled with government contracts.[5]

Those associations that serve more generalized civic purposes are a subset of the general American association pool. Their membership, aspirations and public roles relate to a particular version of ideal citizenship and self-rule. Judith Shklar has focused on energetic citizenship, through both individual actions and social decisions, as a national right and personal necessity. Acts such as voting or expressing a political position generate "a demand for *inclusion* in the polity, an effort to break down barriers to recognition…"[6]

Citizenship's primary benefits in this view feature "agency and empowerment" that draws from both suffrage and the ability to earn and contribute to produce "social standing." Those unable to participate lose societal station on both counts. Associations are highly relevant to Shklar's theory, since they can hold unique potential to activate and enable a representative engagement important both to pluralistic democracy and empowered people.

If civic engagement and assembly are, in theory, national rights, few are acting on the invitation. Leaving aside the difficult question of citizen eligibility, to which volumes could be addressed, there are various counter-forces that obstruct associations' potential to enrich the experience of citizenship. Benjamin Barber and Shklar have both noted strains resulting from America's unforgiving work ethic amidst a declining economy. Volunteerism and civic actions are disregarded because of a general disdain for "leisured" time required to enact self-rule. They have concluded that good civic behavior — association membership included — should be literally rewarded. But enhanced esteem for public citizenship has proved a contentious, if obvious, path because of perceived redistributive and political implications, and has not made obvious headway.

Some associations may appear to oversimplify or manipulate information, sustaining ignorance or tunneled opinion among their membership rather than contributing toward enlarged visions for shared futures.[7] But to presume mentally lazy or prejudicial civic membership is insulting to national character. As Marion Smiley points out, the "language of competence [as a foundation for participation] is inherently antidemocratic," commonly associated with arguments for disenfranchisement at worst or disengagement as a near second.[8]

John Dewey fundamentally disagreed with these dismissive public expectations for civic participation, and promoted associations as key developmental tools for a democratic populace holding little choice but to engage or be overwhelmed by private interests. He promoted the concept of "social intelligence" as the public's potential to grapple with social ills through learned capacity, in turn gained through deliberative vehicles that spurred independent opinion-formation.[9] Dewey's views are fundamental to positive assessment of civic associations and their optimistic expectations for member development.

Just how do associations help members develop? Nancy Rosenblum believes associations' potential to be most significant at the individual behavioral level through encouraging bridging interaction. In that sense, physical membership presence holds prosaic potential to encourage equal-regarding interpersonal relations and a carefully applied "ability to perceive and object to injustice."[10] Amy Gutmann, Dennis Thompson and Claus Offe expect wider impact, arguing that people are capable of mutually reciprocal judgment through assembly that builds deliberative democracy, deriving rationally from intellectual engagement that is "fact-regarding," "future-regarding" and "other-regarding" in pursuit of solutions to collective problems. Anticipating contemporary action within federal agencies to "open" government through practices like online engagement vehicles, Norman Frohlich and Joe A. Oppenheimer have argued that competence can be structurally encouraged if governmental institutions enable enhanced participation, implying that associations can provide the enabling linkage.[11]

In democratic theory, outward-oriented private behavior can therefore translate to publicly-spirited civics "first because it benefits [the citizen] and secondly because it is in part his own work."[12] But while associations can have positive effect, their orientation is frequently oppositional in practice. Many civic groups are highly distrustful of public officials and legislative process. Indeed, history provides memorable examples of civil society and government gone wrong, and institutional distrust can at times be a virtue. But the mismatch between that natural distrust and the trust necessary for a diverse social compact capable of solving its own problems is multiplied by our spiraling contemporary cultural and economic pluralism. In itself, this pluralism provides great depth to our national character as well as particular positive potential for our future paths. But its reality remains highly relevant to the oppositional character, joining motivation and democratic impact of many associations that draw from specific cultural, ethnic or economic societal streams. Observers of these associations' conflicted realm note that their transmission of constant confrontation can directly wound a shared valuation of citizenship, "public" sphere and expanded awareness of "us."[13]

One could therefore argue that people's tendency to associate with like-minded interest groups — associations thick in their midst — is a negative form of democratic engagement. Robert Dahl disagrees. Given inevitable conflict, he has argued that "groups are not a problem for democracy, they are its essence."[14] But while process makes such contestation fair in theory, the unorganized and disengaged need most help. While associations serve both rich and poor, established and disenfranchised, distinctions can be made regarding the character and inclusiveness of the individual action they empower. Warren has noted seven civic virtues that would make the culture of associations — interest advocates or not — more democratically palatable: "A willingness to play by the rules; attuning to the common good; trusting others; empathizing with others; tolerating differences; respecting rights; and deliberating in good faith."[15] As Chapters 4 through 7 will make clear, these elements of a positive "social ecology of associations"[16] provide a high bar that flickers rarely in American history.

An Historical Refresher on Associations in the United States

Associations have fueled a highly volatile and partisan American history. Benjamin Barber's argument that civic associations' fortunes help determine those of democracy is fascinating as a means of interpreting past events and disturbing for the future amidst evidence of current associational decline.

Arthur Schlesinger, Jr. and Theda Skocpol found widespread historical evidence of deliberate association creation and organization by charismatic American leaders to address shared concerns.[17] By the time Alexis de Tocqueville was recording democratic observations in 1830, associations and all levels of government had achieved a mutual dependency enabled by the U.S. postal service, spreading suffrage, evangelistic revivals and the evolving governmental concern that elicited multi-tiered associational program response in correspondence with the federal nature of their governmental "opportunity structure."[18] While many of these federated associations were fraternal and bonding in character, a growing number were bridging social movements that sought value-laden change through well-run webs of commonly-linked people.

Many of the Nineteenth Century historical products of this interdependence have been judged kindly by history. The American Anti-Slavery Society worked with other abolitionist associations to relentlessly push for emancipation of American-based slaves. The National American Women's Suffrage Association was eventually rewarded for its determined, cross-class campaign for women's suffrage. Others are unevenly cherished, like the American Temperance Society, judged by Americans as too invasive and severe, and the Ancient Order of Hibernians, welcoming new Irish immigrants into segmented havens.

Associations' commonly assumed federation structure flourished from 1800 to 1950, providing members with tools to move up in society. Within the decorous, stolid halls of groups like the Freemasons and Hibernians, men and women found identity, companionship, shared values, expanded skills, outward concern, and an integrative capability that weathered an increasingly mobile society. Women's rise to prominence through church and community groups led to otherwise unavailable skill development and influenced associations' energetic moral agenda. These properties positioned associations as "vital agents of democratic revitalization in American history," galvanizing a level of socially concerned engagement that would inspire the Progressives at the turn of the Twentieth Century.[19]

Our contemporary crisis in Tocqueville's cherished associations is not due to their disappearance, but rather to their increasing professionalization, partisanship and passive membership. Theorists like Peter Levine believe a new embrace of volunteerism, public interest and developmental learning through associations can be informed by focusing on the Progressive Era that enlivened philosophy, politics and the social sciences from the turn of the Twentieth Century to the middle of the 1920s.[20] The Progressive movement's uniting reformism challenged public inability to narrow wild discrepancies in income and power issuing from technological profiteering, competing political machines, diverse waves of impoverished immigrants, and widespread presumption of government corruption by a cynical, self-interested but frustrated populace.

The Progressives were an ideologically diverse group largely reflecting the interests of the middle class, disdainful of power abuse from above and disturbed by poverty below. They were convinced the problems arose from powerful economic changes, lagging laws, and latent civic capacity. Frequently evangelistic, they reflected the mores of their time. Their principles, declared in the 1912 Progressive Party platform and mirrored in the 1924 successor, merit explanation for they fueled the optimistic embrace of government to solve social problems and also inspired the reformist intentions of the nascent League of Women Voters. Good government and anti-corruption measures were advocated to strengthen bureaucratic and legislative rules and unseat city bosses threatened by reform. Fair redistribution was pronounced both morally right in post-gilded age America and urgently advisable for averting Bolshevik-era social revolution. Newly developed management science was launched to improve the delivery of an expanding public service sector. Extensions of popular sovereignty through innovations like direct primaries were believed to give the unpredictable populace better chance to advocate in their true interest. Mutability was sought to clarify what they held to be the relative character of truth, even in regard to the Constitution. Advocating widened political equality was in theory revolutionary; it was also politically astute, since the changes cited herein might best be preserved through launching new voting populations from previously excluded ranks. Finally, deliberation could educate the freshly enabled populace to understand and solve the complex public challenges unresolvable through standard competition. Each of these theoretical threads appeared throughout speeches of Progressive heroes such as President Theodore Roosevelt and Senator Robert La Follette. Their arguments continue to resound today.

The Progressives' 1912 and 1924 campaign platforms also remain noteworthy documents because they pragmatically applied the above-listed principles toward a prescient listing of substantive economic, political and social goals that would eventually encompass the mandate of America's emerging welfare state.[21] Of note for this chapter, the Progressive movement bloomed within reformist associations and, it could be argued, returned there to stay. Progressive social movement associations successfully expanded parameters of government concern into family issues like child welfare, contraception, and temperance while also igniting major change on racial integration and extension of suffrage.[22] Capable leaders launched campaigns to start public interest groups such as the League of Women Voters, the National Consumer's League and the American Civil Liberties Union. (The League, in turn adopted the contents of the 1912 Progressive Platform as its inaugural program in the 1920s.) Each group aimed to connect civically concerned citizens with newly empowered government to deliberatively solve problems of principle like inequality, fair play and equal rights in "the public interest." Their leaders considered associations essential for addressing the critical relation between good citizenship and political reform.[23]

From the start, these Twentieth Century public interest groups faced partisan, bonded and angry opposition, threatened by unwelcome forms of change. While the Progressive Era has its enthusiasts, revisionist critics have pointed out that Progressive association-derived reforming efforts did not always proceed as planned. Public interest associations received criticism in the 1920s that the government they enabled produced a soulless, scientific and elitist management of society and disabled local moral capacity.[24] While group leaders and federal administrators intended equitable redistribution, some observers asserted that association-led reforms tended to produce regulation instead, with few recipients appreciating its too-human implementation.[25] Ironically, conservatives would eventually apply a different version of the associational tool to undo enlargement of government handling of social problems, proposing further that the associational allies of destruction could stand in to provide "functional substitutes" for government. But association theory goes in cycles. Benjamin Barber's recent revival of Tocquevillian notions of active associational citizenship is a reminder that the Progressive Movement still inspires cutting edge reform in spite of sometimes valid criticism.[26]

By 2012, the association world has become unrecognizable from the past chapters of bonding, bridging and righteous indignation. World War II began to dislocate local identity and reframe personal aspirations and national rights. The apparent social lull of the 1950s suggested at first that long-standing associations would adapt to percolating social and economic changes. But in fact, the massive cultural, legal and political shifts brought to fruition by the 1960s' Civil Rights Movement had been in motion during the previous decade, as coverage of the League of Women Voters' history will show in Chapter 6. Quickly, traditional motivations to join civic and particularized associations were de-legitimated.[27] The reputations of stalwart chapter-based membership associations like the General Federation of Women's Clubs (GFWC) were durably associated with discriminatory practices. Clout and membership evaporated almost overnight as a result. Most young people of the 1960s and 1970s chose not to join associations considered tainted and passé, seeking linkage with more integrating and contemporary currency. Military support groups, which epitomized the patriotic fervor so common to past association ritual, lost their bridging allure and created generational conflict. As Skocpol observed in a Massachusetts-based study applicable to other regions, these widespread rejections "dissolved much of the moral glue that enabled cross-class associations to flourish, particularly among men."[28] Changing gender rights further reduced members by redirecting highly educated women toward work. Few gender-specific groups survived because of equal rights legislation, though ethnic groups continued to thrive.

The subsequent decades have been volatile. A few longstanding member-driven associations have proven adept at extreme crusading about retirement benefits, teenage fatalities, birth control and guns via direct mail and the web. Like other cocky new players, they have tended to become well-versed in the "business of building membership,"[29] and have developed a vested, specific message that assists their viable contests with other competitively structured groups on a corporate-equivalent playing field, interpersonal bridging potential discarded to the winds.[30]

These new groups are frequently civic in focus, but not in the traditional volunteer manner, for they are professionalized, hierarchical and largely lacking proactive members. They have joined a larger advocacy "explosion" to meet a changed "opportunity structure" of expanded bureaucracy and permissive election regulations. The new "march on Washington" arrives with tools ranging from clipboard-carrying students, direct mail missives, public relations specialists, computer wizards, grassroots phone-bankers and lawyers.[31] Idealistic organizational entrepreneurs continue to operate and some may do so with minimal funds, but most choose to avoid the developmental bottom-up engagement so fundamental to "schools of democracy." Theda Skocpol has asserted that the clear reduction in participatory associations has "diminished democracy" through reorientation of huge civic resources away from hard-won cooperative identities, values and aims. There is increasing evidence that public-oriented membership groups qualify as relics. Skocpol notes, "Summary statistics about 3,000 social welfare and public affairs organizations founded in the 1960s – 1980s show that close to half indicate no 'members' at all, and another quarter claim fewer than 1,000 'members . . . . To borrow the colorful phrase of my colleague and fellow researcher Marshall Ganz, the vast majority of recently founded civic associations are 'bodyless heads."[32] She further observes that rapid shifts in leadership demands, organizational complexities, technology requirements and digitally linked supporters have a profound impact on which organizations will thrive and influence public decisions.[33] More importantly, such competition exacerbates existing inequalities through robbing those under-equipped of equivalent voice.

Who still volunteers in this climate? Many working professionals will either send a donation or remain unaffiliated, offering occasional self-rewarding hours to social service agencies, yet missing out on the moral development from deliberate bridging engagement. But others still show for the Kiwanis' social hour. Researching recent joining patterns in Massachusetts, Skocpol found that while affluent, educated Americans left fraternal and civic organizations in a post-1960s rush, less-educated, military-aspiring Americans stayed.[34] Their loyalty generates flag-carrying citizenship celebration in membership associations like the 4-H Club and the American Legion, yet lacks the bridging benefits of previous eras. A chasm has developed between (a) well-heeled leaders and followers of nonprofit advocacy organizations, sharing common lifestyles regardless of view, and (b) those patriotic upstanding Americans they're ostensibly serving. Careful consideration of "protest businesses" does reveal predominant middle-class orientation, with the less educated and more isolated opting for "hokey" membership in a more traditional vein.

Association Typology

It is becoming apparent that there are significant differences between associations that will affect their public operation and impact. David Knoke has presented "a minimal definition" of an association as "a formally organized named group, most of whose
members — whether persons or organizations — are not financially recompensed for their participation."[35] If only it were so simple.
The categorization of associations is very challenging, in part because of loose terminology.

A reasonable requirement would be the presence of members.
Warren notes that 576,133 tax-exempt membership organizations
were in existence in 1995, not including religious congregations.[36]
But what makes for membership? Certainly some will list very active followers but others may attract those inclined to physically
stay away. Are both fine ways to be a member? Does it count to
simply write the check or must one attend regularly in person and
adhere to rules, activity expectations and shaped norms? How
many members make for a viable roster? Can the simple presence
of members mask an identity not driven by public participation?
These questions are not answered easily.

Must an association be small and local? Tocqueville concluded
so, yet Skocpol later disagreed. While the function and scale of associations vary widely, the more telling detail is how they structure
to accommodate members. Some will have a horizontal self-governing management style that relies on member volunteerism. Others will assume a more professionalized hierarchical organization
yet rely on members for their voice and direction. Warren has argued that an organization's structure will unveil its purpose, with
the first developing its members' abilities and the second streamlin-
ing for advocacy.[37]

Is it reasonable to hope that associations can bridge social and
economic divides through their membership? Certainly, a range of
associations exist that fuel polarization rather than build social capital. Jason Kaufman has considered the historical record of American associations to incline toward exclusionary, nativist, racist, and
incendiary character, permeating civil society and blocking progressive change.[38] Yet other associations like the Masonic Lodges
have clearly bridged class through fraternal orientation, drawing

to common purpose (if imperfectly in racially classified society) people who would otherwise have stayed separate.

Is it realistic to seek associations that forgo narrowly targeted benefits to embrace transformative "public" concern? In fact, many groups will pass this bar. E.E. Schattschneider provided the dividing line:

> Public interest organizations are generally *defined by some end or principle*. Anyone who agrees with their credo can join, although membership may require a moderate fee . . . . Organizations that so readily admit members usually interpret their ends in general terms... Not everyone agrees with their specific agendas, but their aspirations are framed in (formally) universal language... By contrast, the National Association of Manufacturers (NAM) permits only industrial corporations to join. What defines the NAM is not a principle or end, but rather an *identity and the interests that follow from it.*[39]

Public interest groups derive from an earlier "social movement" tradition that flourished within churches and community group to address generalized societal problems. These independent reformist groups represented one third of all associations operating from 1776 to 1955.[40] As described earlier, their public interest form gained stature in the Progressive Era, but they have been experiencing a powerful resurgence since the 1970s. They are frequently categorized as "good government" groups in the sense that they seek to exert change in already existing political processes to improve capacity to solve common problems. In general this associational subsector exhibits pragmatic aims that bear resemblance to original Progressive Party platforms but in contemporary form. They variously combat collective action problems through measures like public journalism, civil investing, social unionism, service learning, civic environmentalism, study circles and deliberative polling. (Founded in 1973, Common Cause is a classic example of the new round of "good government" public interest groups and is widely esteemed for its accomplishments. Environmental groups have also weathered the storm, blending "protest business" and "expressive"

elements to agilely mobilize their membership, defeating on occasion considerable odds.)[41] Though officially nonpartisan and bridging in their marketing, their agenda tends to be more successful in
Democratic administrations. In practice, public interest association
executives can be as integrated into the policy process as sectarian
colleagues, and their management structures are very uneven in
terms of democratic handling of their own members, *to the extent
they have them*. Their principles are sorely tested as they pursue legislative goals. Association theorists are expressing concern that particularly those public interest groups that take membership-based
chapter-federation form lack the necessary technological acuity to
competitively play the current protest game.[42]

Is it fair to term associations, irrespective of "public" orientation, "interest groups in civil society robes?"[43] David B. Truman defined an interest group to be "any group that, on the basis of one
or more shared attitudes makes certain claims upon other groups
in society for the establishment, maintenance, or enhancement of
forms of behavior that are implied by their shared attitudes."[44]
For an individual-based membership association to be included, it
would seek to influence policy but not attempt to govern. Many
associations will fall into this advocacy category. Few theorists
would argue advocacy is necessarily inappropriate. Jordan and
Maloney have posited "pure" membership-based interest groups
to be achievable, made beneficial through proactive bottom-up engagement, accountability and organic life cycles, so long as they
produce democratic norms and civic incentives among members
that in turn influence extended populations. But "ideal" interest
groups draw from a very small member-driven supply. In 1990,
for example, American lobbying groups with members accounted
for only 22.8% of total registered lobbying organizations. An earlier
count found that 70% of "citizen" lobbying groups actually lacked
members.[45]

Associations vary regarding the character of entry. To be democratically beneficial to the member, joining and resigning needs to
be a matter of individual choice. But while many associations scru-
pulously adhere in theory to open invitation, few decisions will be
made in isolation. Unsurprisingly, many resolutions to join will
have been influenced by culture, community and circumstance.

Even for generalized groups that don't set parameters, there will be clusters of similar people. As will be made clear in Chapter 4, the more interesting detail is in the degree of variation.

At first glance, one would expect easy categorization of associations within a nonprofit heading. But this turns out to muddy the definition rather than to hone it. Featuring all organizations not termed profit or government-driven, the nonprofit sector has grown huge, accounting for 7% of the nation's gross domestic product.[46] It is extremely diverse in regard to membership. Certainly there are intimate fraternal groups and counseling circles that rely on participation and affiliation. But there are also nonprofit groups that lobby ferociously with only nominal membership through 501c4 channels. There are also nonprofits that focus on service delivery to beneficiaries in a manner that can resemble successful businesses.

In part because of its functional and structural diversity and also because of a lagging legal response, it is unmistakably true that the American nonprofit sector defies adequate public accountability in both its finances and public impact. In 2008, the National Center for Charitable Statistics (NCCS) noted there were almost 1.57 million nonprofits getting tax-exempt benefits in the United States. Most definitely, these benefits were not distributed according to a civic measuring stick. A wide range of nonprofits qualify for tax-exempt status if they act as charities or "serve broad public purposes in educational, religious, scientific, and artistic fields, . . . as well as the relief of poverty and other public benefit activities" with the general requirement that they spend out a certain portion of their income and adhere to Internal Revenue Service reporting standards.[47] But groups adhere to these standards unevenly and have distinctive interpretations of "broad public purpose." Different levels and forms of tax benefits will apply depending whether or not the nonprofits lobby, but many groups have become adept at manipulating funds between educational and lobbying wings to maximize their voice and reduce their accountability to IRS scrutiny.

Funding trends within the nonprofit sector are also highly uneven. Some nonprofit groups draw funds primarily from member subscriptions and eke through each financial season. Other groups that are established as charitable enterprises have proven highly successful at raising funds in a manner subscription groups can only dream of; some of these on examination will not merit a populist tax-deductible label for their actual achievements.[48] Increasingly, enduring nonprofits — with or without members — blend in professionalized advocacy and can gather massive sums of money from anonymous donors unrelated to membership. To the extent they are member-driven, civic groups will tend to come into the first funding category.

Given the huge diversity under the nonprofit mantle, it is less helpful to focus on civic associations' tax code (unless tailored to fit) than on their longevity, structure, influence and numbers. Associations' most vibrant time could be argued to be post World War I, with years following World War II coming in a near second. As the 1950's advanced, the largest associations were still drawn from sundry women's clubs, the American Legion and the YMCA. But as we have seen, the stable trend overturned in the following decades, with the august General Federation of Women's Clubs declining by 83.1% from 1955 to 1995, followed by the Masons, who lost 69.8% during the same period.[49]

Which member-driven associations are dominant at the present? According to the National Center for Charitable Statistics' report on the ten largest public charities in 2008, only one was a generalized membership organization, the American Civil Liberties Union Foundation, Inc., with almost $200,000,000 of assets and a lengthy, if distant, member roster. The other dominant nonprofits tend to be specific in their populations or interest, including the American Jewish Committee, a membership organization with nominal entrance fees and opportunities to participate; the National Rifle Association Foundation Inc., which does not invite membership but encourages donations while the NRA parent association does seek membership at nominal rates to unleash on election days; and the NAACP Legal Defense and Educational Fund, Inc., which is structured like the NRA with its parent organization accepting the members. In general, the financially successful "membership" associations are sectarian in orientation and in practice avoid active membership, in terms of governance and activities, for greater flexibility in fundraising, lobbying and organization. The League of Women Voters' national income for 2008 would by comparison look local in capacity, encompassing 2.5 % of ACLU's bounty.[50]

Should There Be Differential Treatment?

Return to the relatively blanket treatment of nonprofit organizations — associations included — in the United States. Take it as a given that the nonprofit sector is creative, compassionate, semiindependent, and irreplaceable for significant portions of public education, service and representation. Also take it as a given that the concept of tax exemption for either donee or donor has important positive consequences in terms of enabling a philanthropic and public-focused zone. Both statements in generally being true, it still is valid in a financially strapped era, wherein taxes foregone have a public impact, to question whether there should there be an enhanced civic measuring stick for nonprofit tax benefits and other forms of public incentives or penalties. Are there solid rationales to justify public distinctions among associations even if such moves may interfere with liberalist human development through free choice and Darwinian life cycles? Those who emphasize the merits of pluralism might argue distinctions are dangerous and could constitute political favoritism. But if the public resolves to encourage particular civic habits while discouraging others, distinctions among groups become one tool for ensuring accountability, encouraging excellence and widening their benefits. How particular associations' democratic ecology impacts the public realm should be at the core of such a decision.

In fact, state-drawn distinctions among nonprofit groups in general and associations in particular constitute a project of considerable, if unfinished, duration. What types of state intervention are in play? Mark E. Warren has recorded various forms: the U.S. government can accord freedom to associations and protect them by law (though not formally within the Constitution); it can intervene through regulation, subsidies and income supports; it can directly affect associations' subsistence through tax exemption or penalty; it can nurture them through public-private partnerships; and it can adjust the power ratio through equalizing the playing field.[51]

Regulating judgments are informed by philosophy, law and pragmatism. Nancy Rosenblum has considered associations to present a poor theoretical case for widespread regulation: "The moral uses of pluralism militate for expansive freedom of association and against a strategy of deliberately legislating schools of

virtue by government inducements or legally mandated congruence." While illiberal practice within groups has thrived, "demands
for congruence [are]... psychologically naïve and politically misguided." Channeling Charles Darwin, Rosenblum further believes
that the "dynamic of associations... [forming], joining, schism and
disassociation are as much a part of freedom of association as the
solidity of identification and belonging."[52] Government alliance
with one over others would, she believes, be disastrous and un-
sustainable. Individual choice among a "dense array," in this view,
counters most associations' danger or influence. [53] Minimizing regulation would therefore enable democratic culture through helping
individuals engage difference and develop judgment to counter internal problems through resignation, more penalizing than regulation.[54]

   While Rosenblum's emphasis on freedom to associate is compelling to Americans, there are reasons to reserve blanket application and support wider regulation along the lines set out by Warren. The current associational climate in which wolf-equivalents
compete with respective lambs for attention, resources and results
from a seemingly clueless polity leads to highly uneven promotion
of the norms, deliberation, and resource access traditionally attrib-
uted to associations.[55] Because of this trend, some people challenge
Robert D. Putnam's dirge to receding membership by charging
there are *too many associations*, particularly of sectarian character.[56]
At the very least, those associations that lobby or manage private
and government grants for devolved public services need to make
their funding sources and operations more transparent to the general public.[57] Energetic public monitoring is needed to anticipate
associations' self-interest, insure accountability, and seek equitable
impact.

   Where should the line be drawn? Warren submits that those associations meriting regulation are the ones with power to exclude
or discriminate in the distribution of scarce or public resources,
damaging equal representation in the process.[58] Rosenblum her-
self has advocated regulation for those associations that create or
control citizen competence, though "proponents rarely recommend
enforcing congruence all the way down."[59] Peter Levine believes
regulations merit strengthening across the board to insure those as-

sociations most beneficial to democracy earn favorable treatment.[60] Given the importance of a healthy, engaged civil society and with respect for the earnest work done within many of the groups in question, these intervention tools and criteria call for greater national exposure, development and application. To enable this effort, America needs to rediscover the core of a legitimate democratic culture as expressed through assembly.

3

What Makes an Association Democratically Beneficial?

Political theorists have weighed associations' democratic potential through competing political orientations. Liberals in the philosophical rather than political sense value associations' ability to promote interest; communitarians seek their moral solidarity; and deliberative pluralists encourage their civic invitation. All conclude that some associations are more beneficial than others, and that most only partly embody the ideal. These varied theoretical discussions also tend to agree that the most promising associations are those dying in the people's midst.

There are ten very compelling ways in which associations can be said to create otherwise unavailable democratic effects. It is worth spelling each one out clearly to demonstrate the rarity of associations that meet each criterion. Most groups will excel in some areas and not relate to others.

One group of democratic benefits draws from associations' unique ability to address self-rule through helping citizens to train and activate themselves as empowered participants. Alexis de Tocqueville's famed school for democracy is real for those putting in volunteer time as members.[1] These benefits draw from the readiness to energetically join, the schooling in procedure and substance that results, and the satisfaction of amplified voicing of shared interests.[2]

A second clustering of democratic benefits comes from associations' combative self-interested inclinations. Grant Jordan and William A. Maloney suggest associations' primary impact on democracy is to "to increase the level of contestation over policy."[3] But is that a bad orientation? Maloney has asserted, "self-interest is far from a pathology. If all citizens were motivated solely by regard for others, then it would be likely that their appetite for involvement would quickly evaporate."[4] Moreover, some view self-interest as a public version of self-defense.

A third grouping of benefits is more conditional, positing that associations are democratically beneficial to the extent they improve the "public sphere" through developing quality dialogue between the government and its citizens. Such dialogue enables the formation of informed individual opinion, and enhances legitimacy through engaging citizens in the process of policy.[5] To that end, associations that meet this criterion accept fair rules of procedure, contribute to mutually justifiable debates and legitimately accepted outcomes, and assist in expanding the voices of those affected by public action. Such deliberative merit draws from acceptance of legal and ethical codes, full representation of difference, and accountability for methods, aims and selection of those who participate.[6]

A fourth category refers to associations' frequent orientation toward issues of collective concern. Through incentives, ideals and drive, they hold the potential to resolve thorny public issues through collective action. John Dewey and Carmen Sirianni have referred to this associational prospect as "social learning." Such action permits practical realization of a normative public good that is unachievable on individual terms and requires widespread focused support.[7]

A fifth benefit from associations draws from their interpersonal dynamic, which brings people together to "experience pluralism."[8] This associational encounter transforms judgment toward reciprocal "self-interest properly understood,"[9] improving opinion quality and the resulting representation. It also fundamentally shapes individual moral development in an "expressive" fashion through affecting disposition toward other people, encouraging habits of equality and volunteerism in daily life. As Jordan and Maloney observe, "expressive actions are values of a person or group rather than instrumentally pursuing interests or values... [B]enefits are derived from the expression itself..."[10] Viable membership associations thus promote self-fulfillment of one's values through enabling tangible personal application of shared principle. Potentially, such personal development enlarges personal concern, produces service and sustains the organization, compounding democratic benefits.

A sixth benefit issues from associations' wide and largely unregulated array. Nancy Rosenblum notes that through negative liberty, "forming, joining, splitting and leaving associations are as personally significant as communitarian 'belonging'; indeed, they are a prelude to it."[11] The key to this benefit is unhampered selection. Jordan and Maloney note, "the nature of the democratic choice is in the support itself... Put bluntly, the Schumpeterian democratic choice is between groups. If you do not like the group, do not join it."[12] Freedom to leave if personal and associational goals diverge is an important democratic benefit. Some organizations may promote cooperative ethical and negotiating structure, in which case discord can also provide the choice to stay and mediate. In the process, Rosenblum has concluded that members will learn habits of tolerance, self-discipline and justice.[13]

A seventh benefit of associations comes from their powerful ability to adjust opportunities to both participate and be heard.[14] The wider the partisan splintering of groups, the more tailored the choices of engagement to taste and circumstance. While common opinion may be lost in the process, a wider representation of people may engage through specific associations than would be the case with large-tent presentations. In particular, associations have historically amplified voice for those without traditional political clout, "representing difference" with compelling morally-tinged force.[15]

An eighth benefit of associations comes from their contribution to social capital and trust so important for resolving common issues at any level. Associations help create such trust through bringing different types of people together for common purpose, thereby helping to create social glue necessary to unite a diverse population. Such bridging potential has resided by degree in fraternal groups throughout American history, with active civic membership across class. A population that engages in shared endeavor helps ensure accountability as well as trust, enabling both prosperity and progressive legislation.[16]

A ninth benefit can come from associations' internal structure to the extent they operate democratically and encourage valid member contribution to means and goals.[17] Such groups empower their members with a burgeoning sense of efficacy through giving them a role in decision-making and implementation in a field of personally assigned importance. They further demonstrate an appreciation for individual membership through finding processes that fairly elicit individual views while official positions are being developed. Leadership, modeled on federal democratic practice, is in such cases a mix of grass-root expertise and national guidance. If association structures enable a tiered engagement path that facilitates local as well as general focus, they can help improve a jurisdiction's detailed attention to community and regional needs.[18]

The tenth benefit of associations relates to Tocqueville's belief that democratic countries required shared interests and values — habits of the heart — to enable the reciprocal judgment to help democracy survive and prosper. Such commonality, he submitted, issued from cultural heritage and enabled the voluntary associations to bond the country together. While the concept of homogenous, culturally-derived values has become more problematic in pluralistic contemporary society, at a minimum citizenship itself can only have meaning if a shared valuing of its rights and obligations can be made more available to the general population. Civic associations are frequently oriented to this purpose, holding a special democratic potential.[19]

Can there be negative democratic effects from associations? Absolutely. Each of the above-cited benefits can be turned on its head if conditions take the alternative direction, and discussions of associations' merits are rife with qualifiers. There is evidence that associations can disable deliberation, fair representation, common interests, and political efficacy to solve collective issues. To the extent these malignant seeds take root, they frequently breed from the plummeting prospects for meaningful membership, confusion of means versus ends in a professionalized association culture, illiberal trends in associations within a pluralistic civil society, partisanship dominance over public interest, and the extraordinary inequalities in contemporary America.[20] Such arguments are compelling, but they provide an incomplete forecast of democratic decline. Within the otherwise disappointing contemporary association pool described in Chapter 2, a small number of civic public interest groups are particularly promising in their outsized ability to measure up to the ten democratic associational virtues listed above. The negative national engagement spiral can be stemmed in part through these uniquely participatory associations if they find ways to sustain themselves, a future presently in doubt.

What Makes One Aim More Public Than Another?

Most associations tend to make normative claims to wide-ranging solutions that will reorient a temporarily misguided compass toward the country's "true" values. Americans have traditionally been both leery and susceptible. As far back as 1789, Alexander Hamilton deemed public reasoning to be camouflage for powerful private interests that dangled the "pretext of some public motive" to lull gullible voters into false confidence.[21] D.S. Cupps argued within the twentieth century that virtuous-appearing advocates of "public purpose" were inevitably subjective, advancing their own middle and upper middle class interests.[22] Jordan and Maloney conclude, "Most groups could construct a plausible argument . . . they are acting on behalf of a wider community or that the wider community will benefit from the changes, or goods and benefits they seek."[23]

Some approaches toward public aims are competitively aggregative, suggesting that positions with the most votes are by definition the most public. Yet simple aggregation is increasingly viewed inadequate and immoral as an autonomous directive of communal future amidst uneven voting and interdependent consequences. Even jaded practitioners concede that some aims can be more public than others. A fairer rendering of a public interest might derive from a cost-benefit analysis that addresses the complexity of voices, varying character of costs, shifting time-frames and border-defying results. Other criteria for public character may issue from intersecting values — the vaunted "self interest properly understood" — involving some level of personal transformation through the process of assisting community resolution of privately experienced challenges.

However reached, public-oriented aims can be tenuous. Their reflected interdependence is frequently ill-matched against disproportionately equipped private interests, and it can seem as though greater public will exists to identify public ills than the solutions that might reduce them.[24] Additional challenges are numerous. The "balkanization of public opinion" that issues from contemporary identity politics and non-blending ethnicities appears to make it difficult to be "other-regarding" of those appearing to hold different values.[25] Given diversity, many associations may agree on a common goal but have very different ways to get there.[26] Then there is the matter of precisely who authorized the associations at hand to define "public" needs. Those groups claiming a purified vision frequently lack the equivalent of Moses' burning bush to prove they hold an authorized version of change. Without question, the bulk of voluntary associations are well-intentioned, thoughtfully directed and methodically informed with creative ideas to address various issues. But their very strength is also a limitation on their influence, for they stand apart as a sector from the communities in which they operate and are without formal authority from government, home or the workplace to conduct their efforts. They are therefore reasonably open to challenge regarding who invited them to function as they claim high ground.[27]

Perhaps the greatest challenge to pursuing a public interest comes from public economics, which identifies a public good as "a good or service from whose consumption no group member can be excluded regardless of the level of an individual's contribution toward the provision of that good."[28] Mancur Olson has argued that public goods like clean water exist — the entire academic field of public economics was created to address them — but defy collective action because of rational free-riding behavior. Paying an individual price to achieve a collective goal exceeds the likely personal benefit. From an economist's standpoint, it is irrational to seek a public aim unless compensated with hefty incentives or penalties.[29] Government is in the "business" of providing public goods for that reason, with penalties of public dissatisfaction abounding.

Challenges granted, the process of figuring out methods to overcome collective problems is not a new project.[30] Public goods and needs frequently relate in general form to fiercely cherished national ideals such as free speech, equal opportunity and the pursuit of happiness. So motivation can be guttural and blanketly supportive in theory, yet challenged by dramatically different translation to detail in practice. This combination can excite high emotions that are dangerously destabilizing in the public realm. Preservation of public goods and resolution of public problems takes place within this thicket and is in theory a core raison d'être for both government and associations, even if realization of the public good seems to get bureaucratically lost in the process.

Both in theory and in fact, public aims and goods that do get substantively addressed draw from the country's deliberative process and rule of law. But there is undeniably a huge gap between the theoretical ideal of mutual justifiability, accuracy, and sustainability on one side and the realities of short-term political vision on the other, and the advancement of public goods remains very difficult, rare and evident only in retrospect.[31] Most such milestones feature unique alliances between particular public interest associations, social movements that may power them, and receptive government players, intent for whatever reason on accompanying the high-minded script with construction of specific cooperative sponsorships that permit the time-specific public aim to take enduring legislative form.

How do these public interest groups compel attention? The answer frequently relates in part to the particular breed of their members. Contrary to Mancur Olson's belief that personal investment in collective cause is irrational, public interest groups thrived in the Progressive Era and have since surged since 1970 with members motivated by powerful intangible benefits. David Knoke has observed a mix of expressive incentives that compensate such members for their volunteer time through the excitement of contributing to a morally just cause and valuing the public aims sought over the horizon.[32] Contrary to "rational" expectation, such social movement groups remain widespread in the United States and have scored significant victories toward public causes.[33]

Public interest groups do not speak with unified voice. One reason is that there are a number of viable responses to the question of whether a common good is identifiable or attainable. For Nathan Glazer, the common good is tolerance amidst diversity.[34]

Robert Dahl has argued it exists in procedure rather than product.[35] Amy Gutmann has agreed with both, particularly since conflicting values require compromised outcomes amidst "provisional" truth, yet she has insisted there is moral imperative to seek truth's closest pluralist approximation.[36] Benjamin Barber has suggested that the common good grows from accepting the commonality of the problem since most issues affect countries and continents, not just individuals. Ownership of responsibility – his lauded "us" – would, he believed, fire up the will to imaginatively progress through the challenge.[37] These positions will power different goals and tool boxes, but they all attempt to construct groups that can theoretically argue multiple sides of a policy equation.

A Search for Coherent Democratic Theory on Ideal Association Roles and Behavior

If indeed member-based public interest associations are capable of benefiting democracy, democratic theorists do not necessarily consider them essential or distinct from more general civil society forces. Each of the ten potentially positive association attributes described earlier in this chapter draw from different theoretical strands, yet remain important elements of ideal association behavior and construction. Proponents of deliberative democracy tend to wax enthusiastic about civic associations. Harry C. Boyte has developed a public work model in which engaged process helps negotiate among difference toward John Dewey's vision of a "shared way of life." He expands "an associated idea of citizenship . . . which takes a public work perspective [that] democracy is the way we meet our common challenges and create the common world, the commonwealth."[38] But other deliberative democrats have hedged their bets. A follower of Jürgen Habermas, Jean Cohen is less sure of associations' allure or influence. While they help produce generalized trust through horizontal interpersonal encounter, he contends that associations are ultimately less important to democracy than the "legal norms of procedural fairness, impartiality and justice that give structure to the state and some civil institutions, limit favoritism and arbitrariness, and protect merit [as] the *sine qua non* for society wide 'general trust.'" Cohen urges the development of professional ethics specific to associations to better qualify them as public participants. As part of that effort, Cohen advocates close examination of associations' power, money and media even if the "public glare" in theory makes interaction fair and deliberative contribution more extensive.[39] These points from Cohen will prove vital for conclusions reached about the League of Women Voters in Chapters 7 and 8.

Other theories focus on preferable association structure and relationships in the context of enduring partnerships between government and civil society. Theda Skocpol combines with Marshall Ganz and Ziad Munson to highlight the widespread interdependence of associations and all levels of government. Imitation of federal organization and procedure, widely adopted irrespective of advocacy intent, gave associations legitimacy, stature and vertical form as early as the early 19th century, joining remote cabin-dwellers to the urban organizers who competitively raced against other associations to link them with national political life. In the process, associations matched their citizen engagement, policy promotion and service delivery to the "political opportunity structures" within each federal government office.[40]

Marshall Ganz and Kenneth T. Andrews take a sociological approach toward understanding democratically effective associations, providing models of leadership and internal organization that power highly successful nonprofit organizations. Andrews believes an organization's manner of operation enhances chances to draw members and win morally justifiable cause. Witnessing the phenomenal success of environmental groups like the Sierra Club (gained in part through their hire of his co-author Ganz's expertise), he could be right.[41]

Realistic democratic association theory also has to account for the voluntary sector's frequently vested, massive political power. Political interest group analysts comprise a large and distinct field, featuring Theodore Lowi, David Truman, Robert Dahl and many others. Particularly while political parties presently exercise a fraction of their former influence, associations appear to carry the representative ball, delivering their members' interests to Capital Hill, executive offices, and court chambers. Though interest groups per se are out of fashion because of the appearance of manipulative inequities, associations' civil society mantle does little to mask the same function and result.[42]

Association scholarship has been particularly energetic in response to Olson. Olson's 1965 theory had claimed irrational basis to join a generalized interest organization, wounding such organizations' capacity to solve collective action problems. The rational choice theory was later "expanded" by John Mark Hansen in reference to paradoxical voting patterns. He submitted that "if people are rational . . . and they receive only collective benefits, they will not turn out to vote . . . . The result will be the same whether they participate or not."[43] The dispute has high stakes, for David Hume's "tragedy of the commons" is that if *all* don't join in corrective change, each individually will fail. Theorists have challenged Olson's dreary arguments by acknowledging his explanation for low numbers, but charging his lack of understanding for those who *do* join or vote.

That last point connects to the academic exploration of values and incentives that promote associational engagement in collective issues. Robert H. Salisbury developed an expressive theory of participation in 1969. He wrote, "Expressive actions are values of a person or group. Rather than instrumentally pursuing interests or values, . . . benefits are derived from the expression itself. . . . The reward is in the process of participation itself, not playing a part in successful policy change."[44] David Knoke examines the role of these expressive values — and associated joining trends to be explored in the next chapter — in the context of resource distribution for future generations. Those who care about issues and get involved in policy formation through associations will more likely influence aspects of the political economy than those who withhold commitment. Yet such tangible influence in "the acquisition and allocation of organizational resources to collective objectives" may not be at the core of members' motivation, but rather the general expressive ideals of a commonly held ideal.[45] This apparently conflicted combination allows for both cynicism and idealism to accurately depict associations' aspirations and makeup.

Mark E. Warren concluded in 2001 that the relationship of associations to democracy was inadequate to fuel distinct democratic theory, but enabled democratic health to the extent that more study was required.[46] Two years later, he had revised his position, casting his lot with developmental deliberative democrats: "The deliberative elements of a democracy can only be organized along associational lines and the deliberative publics can only emerge where there exist social bases in voluntary associations."[47] If these elements are judged crucial, as he came to believe, healthy civic membership associations like the League of Women Voters are critical to our democracy.

4

Which People Join Civic Groups and Why?

Political theorists such as Grant Jordan and William A. Maloney have found that people who join civic associations consider the act either in their personal interest (however defined) or in line with the values they hold. In that sense, these members look at membership as an investment.[1] But it is also true that pre-formed attitudes and interests are rarely the sole motivator, since prospective members will likely encounter the skills of entrepreneurial leaders who have learned to dangle motivation. The choices will therefore be both an expression of personal selection and external persuasion.

Particularly in the case of civic associations engaged in public issues, Sidney Verba, Kay Lehman Schlozman and Henry Brady have argued that it matters a great deal for both "voice and equality" who accepts the membership invitation and gets involved.[2] Their civic voluntarism model focuses on the time, money, articulation, expression and recruitment that make engagement more likely and sustainable. Harried members do exist who juggle full-time commitments and limited income with active association membership if they have compelling personal reasons. But in general, joiners do tend to exhibit some degree of education, leisure and disposable income. Such factors have a profound effect on further personal skill development, national policy orientation, and the distribution of future resources that draw from association activities. In that sense, unequal civic association participation presents a critical enhancement of already existing inequalities of voice, opportunity and acceptance of democratic process. These are choices with significant material and theoretical consequences.

Several authors have produced evidence that recruitment practices reinforce segmentation of an already dissonant population. Jason Kaufman has observed that many associations arose in the Nineteenth and Twentieth Centuries to provide lifelines for new immigrants in an otherwise overwhelming, hostile new world. Their natural tendency to reproduce member characteristics presented, in Kaufman's view, "a stark challenge to the argument that associations can help bridge gaps in the social fabric, joining disparate populations together in fellowship and solidarity." Pamela A. Popielarz has contended that organizations systematically compete for members with shared socio-demographic characteristics. Groups would most reliably sustain those new entrants who identified with pre-existing members, consolidating an already existing niche. [3]

Anne Skorkjaer Binderkrantz acknowledges the bonding tendencies referenced above for particularized interest groups. But she disputes their application to those groups dedicated to the public interest, arguing that generalized goals, principles, wide recruitment, and expressive experience draw a consistently wider crowd.[4] Examination of the League of Women Voters in Chapters 6 and 7 will confirm this theory to a degree. But even with a positive assessment of diverse targeting for civic group membership, Verba's point about the time, money and information necessary for active membership leads to the possibility of class bias within civic groups' vision of public interest:

> More public interest groups need not necessarily increase competition; it may mean more of the same . . . . [Elmer Eric] Schattschneider (1966:35) argued that 'the flaw in the pluralist heaven is that the heavenly chorus sings with a strong upper-class accent . . . . Pressure politics is a selective process ill-designed to serve diffuse interests. The system is skewed and loaded, and unbalanced in favor of a fraction of a minority.'[5]

Schattschneider may have a point. But if indeed public interest-oriented membership is class-loaded, it is also valid to point out that many civic group purposes still remain defiantly general. Verba has therefore asserted that skewed participation can actually improve the quality of the discourse: "'A participatory system that over-represents [those who choose to participate] . . . also over-represents the politically informed and tolerant.'"[6] This point draws attention to an important aspect of free choice. Open invitation is an important attribute of a democratically positive culture, but the lack of control over those who choose to join in presents a choice. Do we bemoan those who opt out or do we focus on those who for whatever reason complete the membership form and become active? Increasing numbers of political theorists look intently at the motivation of the latter, in recognition of their outsized democratic role.

Why People Join Associations

What signals individuals' lonely-appearing activation of civic membership within an increasingly disengaged culture? It will likely derive from a blend of personal and public ideals that give competing motivational clues to the receiving organization of choice.[7] To understand the range of reasoning, Robert H. Salisbury has developed an exchange theory of interest groups that describes four kinds of benefits leaders can offer members. Some groups offer material, tangible inducements such as distinctively termed credit cards. Others promise social or "solidary" linkage with like-minded people. Additional groups present purposive invitation to help achieve a policy goal such as preserving northwestern wildlife habitat. Most relevant to the League of Women Voters, some civic associations offer expressive incentives of meaningful volunteer participation as a self-actualizing way to activate one's values through sustained public actions.[8] People will most likely respond to a mix of these incentives to both join in the first place and become durable, active members. This point will be borne out in Chapter 6 by League members, who join because of a combination of social links, shared goals and personal satisfaction from assignments like increasing high school voter registration.

Those members whose decisions are based primarily on tangible self-interest are outside the scope of this book. But civic membership organizations are not immune to self-interest or "solidary" social motivation. Regardless of high-minded rationales, serious-appearing people are capable of selecting membership via extremely personal reasons. Most joiners will be affected by what John Mark Hansen refers to as their "personal webs" of family, extended community, and other societal memberships. These webs will both spawn the values creating the interest and likely alert the entrepreneurial recruiters, referenced earlier in this chapter, who competitively draw those of similar value-orientation in. Such recruitment efforts are very "context sensitive" and encourage both expressive and solidary potential. This element of personal linkage holds obvious tendency toward homogeneity but can also enable unexpected bridging combinations.[9]

With general focus on public interest groups and particular concern for the League of Women Voters in 1960, Helen Gouldner's extensive surveys caused her to conclude that "commitment to the specific values of an organization is distinct from commitment the organization as a whole." In her observation, those who both joined and stayed in the League did so less from their expressed idealism than for the "group cohesiveness, integration, influence and morale."[10] Even the most loyal-appearing members can become disenamored by group operation. This point will be borne out in Chapter 6, which describes the rocky early years of the League, besieged by leadership battles and personal bickering.

Those people who join public interest groups will tend to reference their support for generalized outcomes in order to rationalize their membership. After decades of research, Sidney Verba has submitted that more people are willing to work toward collective ends than elitists and rational choice theorists appreciate.[11] Jane Mansbridge has observed the effective allure of soft incentives such as altruism, duty, power, social standing, reputation, thrill, or satisfaction. Expressive motivation to join can be even more powerful through providing unique opportunity to personally effect change. J.M. Hirschman has therefore disagreed with rational choice theorists that association membership is a cost to be individually assessed, noting that the act of participation is often deemed a considerable personal benefit. Even Mancur Olson has admitted that his rational choice theory is less applicable to generalized groups. It is important to acknowledge that soft incentives tend to provide the foundation for enduring public interest support and the associated underwriting of civic associations.

As noted in Chapter 2, Mark E. Warren contends that members' motivations to join tend to contribute toward an association's management structure.[12] Those people choosing to join hierarchically structured groups frequently do so on behalf of the advocacy made possible through clarity, efficiency and reach. Some members might voluntarily seek groups that feature only nominal participation because they are unwilling to belong on a more active basis. Those organizations with federated structure and active local chapters tend to blend advocacy and developmental member engagement. In that case, retaining the voluntary character of joining and leaving is important for encouraging the positive effects of viable individual participation. In each example, the preferred structure will be reinforced commensurate with the size and intensity of membership.

Once members assemble, a separate management dynamic is launched within the civic association. Organizational theory competes with behavioral analysis of substantive zeal to explain the range of structure, behavior and sustainability that bureaucratically results.[13] A particular aspect of membership associations – not relevant to more streamlined "protest businesses" – is their need for member service, in itself requiring staff that draws resources from program funds. The extent to which member engagement is solicited will be partly affected by internal budget decisions relative to competing organizational needs for efficiency, quality control, and voice purification through centralization and hierarchy. For this reason, association executives are attuned to why members join and will weigh professionalized effectiveness free of volunteers against inclusive invitation to appropriately express appreciation and loyalty, while simultaneously balancing the group's resources toward externally-focused goals.

To the extent that members share sustaining motivation, they might hope for aggregated influence over the association's direction and structure. Such hope can be ill-advised, even when there are significant numbers perceiving solidarity. Mancur Olson has submitted that common intention doesn't translate to common action partly because the "common" frequently gets perverted in the policy and delivery stages.[14] Some organizations misjudge the motivation of their members; others simply disregard them, concluding that new recruitment campaigns would compensate for the products of their autonomous direction. Such disconnect is made more likely by the development of "policy communities" and "mutual dependencies" within public interest associations and the nonprofit sector at large. The sheer number of nonprofit groups with similar ends but highly different means will bend motivations and methods. Reaching for idealistic goals, mini-fiefdoms develop their own bureaucratic needs, social tendencies and practical political alliances. Negative impact will be a far easier product than faithful positive delivery. Those resolutions that *are* achieved will frequently be diluted through compromising incentives to encourage sufficient support among competing groups. Sector accountability for dream failure will often be in short supply. The League of Women Voters' dedication to literal grassroots direction in defiance of these trends will therefore make it unusually responsive to its membership in both management and advocacy.

While some joining motivation for civic membership groups is unmistakably illiberal, Nancy Rosenblum has persuasively argued that government neutrality among associations is critical. She has urged public focus to remain on the free conditions of joining and withdrawing, which in motion should provide "'relatively benign outlets for . . . narrow self-interested behavior.'"[15] If such a stance happens to constrain numbers, perhaps the motivations that forestall membership, public-interested or otherwise, are valid. Olson's position in regard to generalized groups, for example, is that a rational person will see the operational folly. But other reasons to remain disengaged may apply, such as individual dissatisfaction with choices, insufficient funds (membership always involves some form of personal cost), irrelevance of tax-deductibility, constrained time, or lack of certainty that membership would contribute to positive outcome.[16] If bad choices exist, surely the decision to avoid them can be celebrated as civically beneficial.

Those who take the civic plunge to join public interest-oriented groups tend to be a distinct breed. Jordan and Maloney have associated "the 'committed' with an ability and willingness to afford the subscription, a high sense of personal efficacy and a closely-held belief in the [value] of the group and [its preferred] participation."[17] It is important to underline Sidney Verba's point that this general civic membership pattern immerses more deeply a group already inclined to vote and deliberate. The representative impact of members' enhanced voice will be affected by whether one agrees with Schattschneider or Verba that bias can be a good thing.

The problem for our democratic culture is that associations' current joining trends are distinctly going in the private direction in terms of both numbers of contributors and relative wealth of operative groups. Interest groups tenuously carrying membership labels have exploded in numbers. Most of them serve particular interests and operate remote from their contributors. While political parties remain in decline and associations provide the most available engagement vehicle, it is distinctly worrisome that these privately-driven groups have so many supporters. They are highly influential in securing inequitable versions of "public" outcome yet appear impenetrably vague in composition and direction. Matthew Crenson and Benjamin Ginsberg have credited the accelerating associational trend toward "privatization" of American democracy as directly responsible for widespread citizen alienation from public life through robbing their motivation to join in civic life.[18] Public accountability is inadequate in terms of both disclosing donors and clarifying impact of this shifting independent sector. Absent a legal structure that adequately governs the nonprofit sector, associations can be either a feeble attempt at self-rule or an audacious pretense of engagement in a nonpublic "democratic" government.

Civic associations like the League of Women Voters consider the surge of a professionalized and particularized association environment to present serious challenges to equitable and deliberative democratic self-rule. They therefore support reformed rules for the entire nonprofit sector and exhort citizens to examine groups carefully before joining.[19] Perhaps unsurprisingly, these sensible positions are viewed as highly political given the resources at stake, yet their theoretical rationale is compelling for a country priding itself on equal and fair opportunity.

5

What Nurtures, Compromises or Erases
Civic Association Operation?

Equal deference to particularized associations is not featured in this assessment of future prospects for democratically beneficial civic associations. Specific and vested interest groups, with or without members, will undeniably continue to thrive, dragging down deliberative engagement in the process. My concern is rather directed toward those relatively small civic groups of public interest orientation. These entities have been found within Chapters 2 through 4 to have unique democratic importance for developing individual understanding of their public roles and responsibilities in American democracy. The fact that they are struggling as a sub-sector is therefore cause for considerable alarm about narrowed public judgment and hijacked self-rule in their absence. But it would be premature to predict their total demise, for civic groups have significant tools and trends in their favor. The first step to improving their theoretically critical prospects is to understand the operational character of their current problems.

One issue is predictably the lack of money within many civic groups' coffers. To operate, they need funds to hospitably support quality programs and research that will reward their membership and fuel an informed voice. In this area, public interest associations suffer from the vastly higher sums available to particularized organizations. Private money does exist to solve collective problems the public won't fund, but Americans prefer to give it away to selective populations rather than addressing the totality. As evidence of these long-lasting trends, the number of national charities has increased by 63.7% from 1999 to 2009, with a huge combined treasury in the trillions that dwarfs civic groups' hand-to-mouth draw.[1] Americans seem to be confirming Alexis de Tocqueville's Nineteenth Century observation that they will contract out almost anything in a fashion that makes them feel good. Such segmented generosity is passive, since the only action required is making the gift.

Another problem is undeniable. Fewer people are joining bridging civic associations. In fact, *these associations are gradually disappearing.* From 1999 to 2009, participatory civic leagues, social welfare organizations, and local associations of employees (a big chunk of the category) fell by 10.4% to a tenuous 111,849 groups throughout the country, representing 7.1% of all national nonprofits and 3% of charities' income.[2] Those that do survive may do so through offering to shoulder the burden of community task completion, draining some self-help capacity otherwise required for viable communal life.

Mancur Olson's free-rider problem described in Chapter 4 provides another challenge. It seems established that most people who are considering association membership will not choose public interest groups, preferring others to carry the generalized burden and limiting their commitments toward more direct personal gain. Peter Levine has observed, "Even in the heyday of the 1970s, groups like Common Cause and Public Citizen managed to recruit much less than 1% of the American people – mostly wealthy individuals for whom a $20 membership fee was a negligible expense. Meanwhile (as Olson's theory might have predicted), commercial organizations were able to overcome the free rider problem by spending money. Companies could stir up "grassroots" pressure, and media figures could boost their ratings by disseminating political messages."[3] These trends have enabled a manipulative dynamic that positions wealthy individuals to contract out "participation" on public issues that bears little relation to grassroots sentiment. In the face of biased media and big money, civic groups with public interest orientation find it difficult to compete.

The lack of fairness on the public playing field poses ethical challenges for viable civic methodology and goals. Judging by the popularity of particularized groups like the American Freedom Riders, extremism appears to increase membership and media attention. But generalized civic groups have increasingly responded by channeling their Progressive forebears to target such "special interests" on behalf of less-represented populations. Peter Levine notes that political support for these equitable representations of arguably majority-scale needs is ironically crippled by reformist election-cleansing issuing from the Progressive Era, which leashes political parties and unions and, in his view, "undermines the very institutions that had been most loyal to ordinary people."[4]

Meanwhile, many nonprofit compatriots have shifted their missions away from independent action in favor of the rewarding area of federal contracting to perform publicly authorized services. In 2001, the federal government funded one third of the independent sector's operations.[5] This practice has compensated for some civic associations' declining membership dues, but it also discourages a measure of volunteering and breeds uncomfortably intimate government relations already compromised by increasing lobbying from groups with 501c4 designation. The precious normative associational appeal of independence is losing a measure of its credibility with the public as a result. (Note that the League of Women Voters is a stalwart exception to this practice, refusing government funds for all operations except international diplomacy.)

Civic association survival is also impacted by the traditionally short public attention toward matters of principle and the quickly shifting moral standards of our time. Progressive associations suffered from this tendency in the 1920s when President Woodrow Wilson misjudged the public's readiness for further reform; his citizens wanted speakeasies and shortened hems instead, and fled from earnest association attempts to improve their communities. Historians have found that expressive social movement groups like the National Organization for Women are easy to start but harder to sustain and strengthen because of fickle public reception of their values-bound mission. Robert H. Salisbury observed in 1969 that some association leaders appeared to gamble with members' idealism to advance organizational stature, lobbying for generalized purposes when their membership was high and particularizing them as the numbers dropped, with the shifts providing profit or deficit in leader discretion separate from member control.[6] Clearly, to the extent an association is to be democratically beneficial, such shifts in value base may seem sustainably expedient but could produce member resignation. Expressive groups need to be alert to the management tenor of the leaders they develop. Particularized interests gain in this climate, powered with tangible benefits to win the day while disheartened idealists retire.[7]

An additional issue is that some practitioners see public interest membership groups as an expensive luxury in comparison to the preponderance of groups in "protest business" mode. Embracing centralized authority has allowed these latter nonprofit professionals to update time-honored hierarchical methods in order to evolve into skilled lobbyists fueled mainly by "checkbook participation" to reach the advocacy home-plate. [8] It is difficult to validate legitimate democratic benefits of association membership if the supporters show their civic behavior solely through financial support. Increasing numbers of associations weigh whether it is beneficial to carry *any* active members, and find that fundraising could easily recoup the equivalent pittance from membership dues.[9] The member engagement that Chapter 3 found to be so beneficial to American civil society brings sizeable costs through dedicated staff time and space; it may also dilute the professional image and confuse the policy direction. In this competitive climate, Grant Jordan and William A. Maloney consider it worthwhile to provide extensive provocative argument for the view that members may have become superfluous.[10] Have members and internal democracy become "'non-lucrative distraction[s]?'"[11] The answer in terms of both democratic theory and application is a resounding no. While some democratic potential exists in an association's well stated, professionally rendered policy position, the distinctly undemocratic methods associated with the predominantly hierarchical management that accompanies such professionalism increasingly exclude citizens from the public sphere in one of the few remaining vehicles for personal citizen development.

On a practical level, members and dollars for all associations are finite no matter how weighty the related public issues may be. Jason Kaufman has noted the "competitive dynamics of widespread volunteerism."[12]   Because individuals have limited time, money and energy, there is a natural limit to the number and diversity of organizations likely to flourish simultaneously. Sociologists refer to this as *organizational ecology*, or the way in which organizations interact with one another in competition for finite resources and opportunities. It is inevitable that some groups will flourish and others will pass from active operation.

On the positive side, many scholars and tacticians have addressed how civic groups of public interest orientation can survive the brutal current competition of finances and values in appreciation that such groups are among the finest jewels in democracy's social capital crown. As a largely positive example of methods which promote continued civic group operation, social organizing is emerging as a proactive academic field that blends sociology, public administration and political theory to explore practical models of successful social change. Academics like Marshal Ganz, Theda Skocpol and Kenneth T. Andrews have discovered that successful recipes tend to be complex. They adroitly tap context, develop member skills, creatively identify new resources, flexibly evolve organizational practices, shift group density, energize membership, encourage teamwork and insist on program quality. [13]

Though social organizing's methodology appears daunting, the recipe is most definitely doable through deliberate orchestration. The most consistent ingredient in successful turnarounds is insistence on superb, self-driven, and idealistic leaders with a savvy practical sense, committed to building common purpose by accepted rules in order to spawn social change.[14] Hardly Bolshevik egomaniacs, these people are organizational entrepreneurs from the original federated association mold of the Nineteenth Century, skilled in motivating and empowering other people and infused with authority to keep the organizational rudder straight and effective.[15] Associations need to invest in such multi-level leadership development to insure both current and future success.[16]

An additional method for improving sustainability of civic groups is for association leaders to take a page out of the "protest business" playbook, addressing success as a science. Relevant business models have been developed, such as *Enterprising Nonprofits: A Toolkit for Social Entrepreneurs*[17] which help association executives to balance membership demands with the achievement of maximum impact via minimal resources. It is reasonable to suggest that such skills come from tough experience more than textbooks, but "organizational studies" in some cases may help make the appropriate judgments.[18] Many associations therefore draw from professional organizers to periodically cleanse and reenergize their operations.

As David Knoke has observed, public interest associations have a highly complex job of funding and delivering connection, activity and advocacy.[19] Technology has become indispensable for achieving that balance, and can permit incredible activity to generate from few people. Rejecting the indispensable tools of Internet and computers is not an option, and investment in equipment and expertise is critical. But there is a risk in this currency, since many civic associations represent populations lacking computer access. The challenge will be to avoid become remote and elite in order to sustain operation.

Increasingly, medium to large-scale civic associations need professional fundraisers to support themselves in a competitive environment. Dues are set at levels that require supplements from grants and general solicitations. Most associations draw from experience to anticipate fluctuation on all levels and limit their dependence on membership dues in the revenue balance. Environmental groups, for example, count on membership fees for a range of 32 to 38% of revenue, with the balance derived from grants, contracts and corporate gifts. The League of Women Voters falls within the same range; its membership funds represented 35% of its total funding in 2009.[20]

Direct mail provides an additional and apparently irresistible tool to supplement income and solicit new members. But while the popular practice permits widespread message dispersal and increases, by degree, groups' membership and funding, over-reliance on this measure should be cautioned. Its widespread use is very expensive, taking as much as 48 cents from ever dollar raised for past and future fundraising costs. It also builds a development bureaucracy in the process, which can be viewed as controversial when donors comparison-shop overhead rates among prospective groups.[21]

There is a separate issue with direct mail that should be considered regardless of its financial pull, for it inevitably narrows the ideally general audiences for civic associations through the use of targeted lists. Jordan and Maloney observe that as a result, "groups focus their efforts not on those who need *most* persuading but on those whose support they are most likely to obtain." They reference a 1988 study by R. K. Godwin on a resulting practice of reinforced exclusion "because [the excluded groups] lack the discretionary income and political interest to subscribe to news magazines or donate to the causes that would place them on [the] prospecting list."[22] Those already less served democratically will not be prospected.

Jordan and Maloney suggest that direct mail may have reached its saturation point with both anonymous and loyal recipients.[23] While a possible decrease in direct mail effectiveness might hurt civic associations in the short run, in the long run a shift from the practice could be a gift of large proportions. Its missives endanger trust-enabled public interest through extreme messaging; the most successful campaigns thrive by accentuating urgent danger and "immediate" response, breeding distrust of "the enemy" as a result. Unfortunately, a greater likelihood is that the practice will continue via email rather than the U.S. Postal Service.

Recruitment is often an energetic organizational investment in anticipation of membership turnovers. Like their sector-specific association brethren, civic associations engage in market analysis of those most likely to join and "rationally" skew recruitment campaigns accordingly. This methodology, though imperfect for social capital, tends to be predictive and can even be positive through activating passive members with inclination to act in the public interest.[24] But in the targeting process, it behooves civic associations to consider those who aren't on the official "trolling" list and to try to widen their recruiting practices by additional means to allow for greater diversity.[25]

Declining membership does not always signal immediate concern, since many civic associations judge second-year drop-out rates between 30 and 40% to be normal.[26] But stalwart members are consistently more central to group effectiveness than numerous transitional contributors. Association specialists such as Helen Gouldner and Robert H. Salisbury have found that such loyalty is achieved through internal democratic structure and well-matched social, purposive, tangible and expressive incentives.[27] Kindergarten-equivalent manuals for these groups might be helpful as well, since even the most loyal members are capable of developing apparently irrational gripes with their associates. Personal readiness to share the podium will help sustain lasting success, a common challenge for those seeking to change the world. (The League of Women Voters will feature among groups that exhibit this vulnerability.)

Civic groups of public interest orientation definitely benefit from the fact that their members have great faith in active developmental enablement. These individuals frequently exhibit sincere aspiration toward leadership and deliberative understanding as a means to resolve collective problems.[28] James Madison himself might have found them to be ideal citizens. But skeptics might wonder whether such enthusiasm is sustainable. Examples like the 2008 Democratic Party campaign can occur, breeding bridged, infectious volunteerism on a large scale that seems to bestow legitimacy in its wake. But the question for later cycles is whether that type of enthusiastic engagement can be revived. Professional organizers will improve such prospects through making volunteer efforts compelling, personally relevant, and at some level enjoyable. Their professional involvement can produce tangible return from volunteer activation, as engagement can translate to financial commitment.

Some Twenty-first Century innovators are calling for re-adoption of the old confederated model as a means to revive associations' roles in democracy. Peter Levine, for example, has suggested that such retroactive innovation of centrally guided local chapters was key to Christian Coalition success in the 1990s and is, by competitive emulation, re-entering the progressive public interest sphere as a civic teaching model.

Since the chapter structure requires myriad presidents, secretaries and treasurers, it teaches leadership skills to members who may lack alternative development channels. This argument is borne out by the otherwise unavailable skills American women developed during the Nineteenth Century within suffrage and abolition associations. Chapters also bring people together from far and near to act cooperatively, thereby building complex social capital. Because chapters of different organizations can meet and share resources, they may increase the overall capacity of their communities to solve problems. Finally, chapters acquire power and information, so they can sometimes hold their own national organizations accountable.[29]

John D. McCarthy focuses on a different dimension of federated structures. He argues federated structures have been historically popular because they are effective. Especially in relation to social change movements, federated groups "use the concept of franchising — well-developed in the replication of units . . . to think about the reproduction of chapters of local social movement organizations (SMOs) based on national movement models."[30] Through making it easier for people to combine effectively, confederated structure can possibly provide a gift to those who care about the survival of civic associations as a component of American democracy.

Those civic associations that have weathered the cultural storm alluded to in Chapter 2 have been innovative about pushing their membership envelope to emerging generations. Jordan and Maloney have recorded the shifts from boom to bust and sense that people may be surprisingly ripe for renewed invitation to actively engage in volunteer groups.[31] They point out that the business of mobilization is rapidly changing, blending new forms of professional and volunteer methodology. The most creative and democratically important development comes from widening the recruitment pool through grassroots approach. There were, for example, 1.5 million highly active volunteers in the 2008 Obama campaign, driven by internet, phone, personal and media-delivered invitation, with technology attendant to maximize affirmative door-to-door electoral response. These details are becoming standard to professional organizers' jobs, and are presently in standard use by Republican candidates as well. Association success stories are rare if they don't feature some version of this creative outreach in their recruitment of new populations.

Civic associations are increasingly banding together for effect, vindicating John Dewey's Progressive faith — despite the post-World War I materialism that affected his times — that "social intelligence" is possible in pursuit of idealistic goals. To the extent they share aims, and many of them do, groups addressing common issues like water pollution bring varying expertise, audience and tools to carry the generalized power of the argument to wider spectrums of people. Their reputations range from conservative to liberal orientation, giving people opportunity to choose a tone yet share a larger goal, successfully raising public awareness and occasional legislative victory through pragmatism in an otherwise impossible climate.[32] The League of Women Voters' alliance with feminist groups during the Equal Rights Amendment campaign described in Chapter 6 will provide an excellent example of this "social intelligence" in action.

But while such alliances do occur, inter-associational relations are also highly competitive for members, dollars and attention.[33] Communities will embrace or reject particular association messages in consumer fashion, seeking local fit. Within this social ecology, civic associations have strong incentive to dangle a deliberately crafted local hook to lure individuals and communities. The message may relate as much to public relations finesse as to valid perception of local public interest. Those groups "still on the shelf" in terms of membership foresworn have lost that brutal popularity contest.

Civic associations like the League of Women Voters have historically added to their authority and legacy through helping the American government resolve public issues. As evidenced, for example, by their early involvement in the Environmental Movement in the 1960s, the League's ability to activate public servants' interest in building public goods can produce the critical votes behind non-particularized legislation. With some historical basis for progressive headway through alliance, it can in that sense appear counterproductive to have combat and distrust as default association mode. But Jordan and Maloney caution, "groups who depend on a membership that receives no selective material rewards must stick close to the protest mode. In effect, they are selling protest."[34] That reformative urge is to reject the present in favor of an improved future. Returning to the Environmental Movement, the early optimism of groups like the League and the Sierra Club shifted to impatient challenge as they considered government over time to be culpable for spurring inaction rather than needed change. In general, civic associations tend to exhort all participants for change and reform. It is not their role to appear satisfied, particularly if they want their members' enthusiastic renewals.

Confederated civic groups hold unique political influence beyond their aggregated members as they identify these moments for combined action. The members who choose to engage in their cause are frequently highly articulate, possessed of campaigning ardor and empowered further through their involvement. As exhibited by soaring public estimation of the League of Women Voters during its heyday in the 1960s (see Chapter 6), the generalized aims that tend to motivate civic association commitment arguably produce higher levels of public respect that can impress constituents and congressmen.[35] These intrepid, occasionally sneaker-shoed crusaders show with regularity and force at their congressman's door, well versed in the federal shape of their associations' "opportunity structure."

As civic associations manage their sustainability in the current volatile world, it is critical for them to protect their normative public interest core. In particular, their expressive function that enables active volunteers to live their values through participation is positive whether or not the aim is reached through the simple act of encouraging the public act of volunteering. This active process connects individuals into the organization's soul, but it may not be available to all members. In order to be beneficial in Nancy Rosenblum's prosaic sense, associations need to guard against activating only the competent or politically correct. It is unavoidable that members will bring different qualifications, opinions and manners to the table. It is also likely that some will choose to forego active roles. While associations should not be held responsible for herculean civic transformation efforts, they will be repaid with enthusiasm and impact to the extent they advance personal development within their ranks and find ways to link engagement with organizational benefit. To the extent diversity deepens perceptions on individual and organizational levels, members' separate motivations are less important than their presence within the group. To achieve a representative mix, associations need to provide a mix of public and private incentives to join, thereby creating a balance of views and a deliberated generalized "better good."[36]

Association theorists document fast-moving sector evolution among civic groups. Decisions made to enable survival may shift end-goals and member characteristics beyond recognition. If fortunate combination of management science, circumstance and determination permit the realization of long-term aims, associations may face unusual opportunities to pronounce their battle won and disband. On the other hand, new generational choices among associations may render some of the previous leading groups obsolete. Whichever scenario faces particular associations like the League of Women Voters, they all are addressing changing prospects that are only partly controllable. When the dust momentarily settles, a wide and largely unregulated associational array is likely to remain, but the roster will have changed. It is important for association advocates to acknowledge the force of this competitive freedom even as they examine emerging vehicles for democratic impact.

Do Current Civic Engagement Trends Matter?

There is a range of disagreement on whether individual engagement in associations has generally gone up or down. Robert D. Putnam contends that there has been a dramatic drop in joining across the civil society spectrum, with correlated implosion of national social capital. Other theorists like Jean Cohen have argued that the manner of joining and mission of associations have merely evolved with shifting culture and technology to take different form in healthy numbers.[37] But within that discussion, few would disagree that civic groups with public interest orientation and viable membership have indeed declined while professionally-run advocacy groups of either generalized or sectarian character are thriving.[38] Some argue that the professionalized advocacy trend within civil society is actually healthy. Michael Schudson, for example, urges avoidance of nostalgia toward a fictionally bonded past, arguing that the new forms of engagement continue to provide civic opportunity for a new multi-tasking era. He advocates "ordinary but not heroic efforts at information gathering and civic participation" that benefit from advocacy groups' cues and information to make optimal public judgments among competing demands.[39] Putnam in turn accepts the argument that shifts in structure and intent preserve *overall* association activity, but also asserts that engagement in its present form derails national civic capacity.

My argument is not that direct-mail organizations are morally evil or politically ineffective. It may be more efficient technically for us to hire other people to act for us politically. However, such organizations provide neither connectedness among members nor direct engagement in civic give-and-take, and they certainly do not represent 'participatory democracy.' Citizenship by proxy is an oxymoron.[40]

Do fewer members "diminish" democratic opportunity? The dominance of particularized advocacy does present major democratic challenge to a country reeling with social and economic inequality amid cultural pluralism. The predictably unequal power of interest groups causes great anger and distrust among some sectors that bleed into other legitimately public issues, ensuring higher rates of coercive government action.[41] While the United States is highly diverse, Theda Skocpol submits its thriving professional associations do not represent that pluralism, arising as they do from oligarchic investments that benefit segments of the middle and upper classes. As a result, she believes American politics focus mainly on "post-material" issues connected to "values" and lifestyle. Tax-exempt funding of nonprofits and foundations lacks accountability as it powers a spiraling increase in unbalanced political voice.[42]

Yet there is a curious counterbalance at play. Peter Levine and Putnam have observed a clear correlation between association membership and those who vote.[43] Who remain as active members? If Skocpol's Massachusetts study referenced in Chapter 2 is correct, they may frequently be those increasingly isolated members of the lower middle class, preserving membership within traditional associations like the Lions Club and remaining staunch in views that lack previous chapters' cross-class deliberation.[44] As Mark E. Warren has found, homogeneous groups tend to reduce the diversity still present, promoting an undemocratic version of member views and further isolating those already without voice.[45] These narrowly formed groups frequently do exhibit active voting rates and are highly capable of producing confounding results for the member-less advocacy groups that appeared to have won the pre-election debate. Professionally run groups, it turns out, are less capable of predicting "member" turnout on voting day. This combination serves to make prospects for deliberative democracy and cross-class legislation very difficult.

Noting rare exceptions such as the enduring voluntary associations within the impoverished state of Maine, Skocpol suggests that past associational trends are largely irretrievable, imperfect and — addressing Maine — lacking in current potential to create prosperity.[46] While associations persist in America, their new forms challenge equitable representation. Given the high stakes for workable government, problem resolution and, particularly, viable self-rule, it is becoming increasingly urgent to reform the voluntary sector that remains to allow for healthy use of the prevailing forms of combination and to encourage survival of those forms most beneficial to democracy.

Returning to a point made within Chapter 2, America's current urge to combine can be made more positive if a wider population is thereby empowered and rules of engagement are made fairer. To achieve that end, Skocpol has therefore called for close examination of the unavoidably interdependent relationship between associations and government. She particularly urges the creation of a national standard for service delivery to lessen the impervious lack of accountability for many groups. In addition, she has advocated favorable tax treatment and subsidized media time for those associations that legitimately activate and empower class-bridging members. Finally, she has agreed with Judith Shklar that citizenship needs higher public recognition to encourage individual valuation of national rights, thereby advocating public voting day holidays and other measures that increase widespread engagement in moments of democratic decision.[47] All of these measures would help civic associations.

Levine — in self-proclaimed Progressive fashion —believes that the democratic impact of current and future forms of combination will be enhanced to the extent legislative and executive means are authorized to shift the balance more favorably toward civic groups with public interest orientation. He therefore argues compellingly against neutrality and for wide-ranging government intervention on behalf of civic associations like the League of Women Voters. His prescription for nonprofit sector reform includes heightened government ethics and accountability; general tax reform; vouchers to publicly encourage volunteerism and the formation of new associations; more grassroots deliberation; expanded public money for public functions; reorienting the media toward its public role; revising tax benefits and penalties for voluntary associations contingent on civic contribution; and examining professionalized public interest groups' usage of "membership."[48] Application of these tools could indeed help determine whether public interest groups will continue to be in the democratic mix. But it is also possible that they will be judged too partisan in impact to legislatively move forward. Shklar's enhanced "citizenship" may have a more neutral and viable ring. For further consideration of corrective measures, refer to the Conclusion contained in Chapter 8.

Part II

The League's Promise

6

The League of Women Voters' Historical Development as a "Congenial Forum for Change"

Shifting to consideration of the League of Women Voters within an evolutionary frame, readers should carry forward theoretical indicators of democratically beneficial public interest groups. Drawing from Mark E. Warren, a healthy "democratic associational ecology" is produced by a range of democratic criteria.[1] Chapter 3 of this work described the following association measures: representing tailored interest; training for active responsible citizenship; improving public knowledge; contributing to public problem resolution; allowing for the experience of diversity; inviting the exercise of free choice; widening diverse public voice; creating social capital through combined activity; empowering personal growth through engagement in democratic process; and encouraging shared values that contribute to public policy.

Whether the League's origins and subsequent history measure up to these highly challenging standards will be suggested by characteristics of its leaders and members; its development of purpose, structure and process; deliberate selection of operational style; reaction to shifting culture; and circuitous trajectory toward organizational strength. Fortunately, the story is interesting, with great characters, laudable plans, human judgments and direct historical intersection with familiar events to encourage those less concerned with democracy and the League to read on regardless. Historical context will link closely to the League's distinctive associational focus on process and expressive values. This chapter will examine how the organization's singular "congenial" public image as a "forum for change" will directly impact its internal and external democratic potential.[2]

Suffrage Origins

The historical expansion of American enfranchisement, predating 1776 to the present, has repeatedly swung between sudden liberalization and fierce, seemingly unstoppable, retrenchment. Causal factors for this volatile movement have included societal response to war, frontier settlement, political competition, urbanization, class conflict, immigration, acceptance of personal advocacy, and spread of faith in democratic ideals.[3] The oscillating protection of evolving voting rights continues through 2012, hyper-political in an age of razor-thin electoral margins. Only those with healthy patience, solid determination, considerable skill and historical luck advance the gradual progress surviving the swings.

Women held bounteous patience and resolve in the decades prior to 1920. They were by far the largest group of excluded voters in the United States when they began their association-driven effort to win the right to vote in 1848. The faded, staged photos that survive their suffrage era ill-describe the bravery, determination and sacrifice of the women who engaged in one of America's toughest fights for self-rule, well aware they were on familiar historical ground. Carrie Chapman Catt, president of the National American Women's Suffrage Association (NAWSA) and later the founder of the League of Women Voters, would comment post-ratification that female suffrage's seventy-two year effort had involved 56 referendum efforts targeting male voters in addition to "'480 campaigns to get Legislatures to submit suffrage amendments to voters, 47 campaigns to get constitutional conventions to include woman suffrage planks, 30 campaigns to get presidential party campaigns to include woman suffrage planks in party platforms and 19 campaigns with 19 successive Congresses.'"[4] Stumped along the way by the Civil War, nativism, economic swings and morality wars, suffragists like Catt learned the mighty lessons of persuasion, veiled power, circumspect alliance and female solidarity as they fashioned a winning strategy.

Exponential suffrage momentum came in the early Twentieth Century with the widening of class representation, increasingly assertive tactics, and a well-managed federation infrastructure among campaigning associations. A wide range of tools helped the movement crest and win, including leaflets, petitions, speeches, editorials, parades, pageants, spectacles, rallies and, with the advent of the National Woman's Party (NWP), demonstrations, arrests and shock-value. While few activists applauded all approaches, the combined effect worked to increase women's suffrage state by state.[5]

The women who powered this long progression toward suffrage ratification were extraordinary pioneers, featuring ministers, labor activists, journalists, doctors and teachers. Carrie Chapman Catt, president of NAWSA's cresting two million members, was a stalwart visionary as well — particularly as an association bureaucrat, personally establishing the confederated structure that enabled organized mobilization to weather the decades toward 1920. The Civil War era had produced tensions between abolition and feminist missions, tactics and alliances that splintered women's suffrage groups for decades. Catt and Susan B. Anthony managed to broker a peace that merged the American Women's Suffrage Association and the National Woman's Suffrage Association into NAWSA in 1890. Catt in particular responded to the consolidation's challenge through diversifying membership, building coalitions and muscling out a grassroots membership structure that could lobby all levels of community and government.[6]

In parallel but divorced track to NAWSA, Alice Paul brought remarkable courage, resolve and British suffragette inspiration to the National Woman's Party's role in the Twentieth Century chapter of the suffrage fight and succeeded in gaining daily, sometimes distinctly angry, national attention. Following President Woodrow Wilson's declaration of war against Germany and Austria in 1917, she and her NWP cohorts began a provocative, occasionally violent campaign against Wilson with hunger strikes, effigy burnings, property destruction and virulent public attacks on his reputation and actions. They were repeatedly arrested and imprisoned on flimsy charge during Wilson's administration, and were force-fed and beaten in prison. One could plausibly argue that it was NWP's extreme tactics that eventually exhausted the country and caused Wilson to shift toward suffrage support rather than suffering personal international embarrassment for democratic suppression at home while promoting democracy abroad.[7]

Female suffrage was clinched with Tennessee's ratification of the Nineteenth Amendment on August 18, 1920. At this point, the majority view was that NAWSA and its moderate predecessors held most credit for gaining the widespread mainstream support for the female suffrage cause that made legislative passage possible. Personally adamant that NAWSA's structure and "front-door lobbying" held closer claim to victory than Alice Paul's theatrics within the NWP, Carrie Chapman Catt urged the former's final convention on March 24, 1919 to "finish the fight" against disenfranchisement through converting its identity to a new League of Women Voters, dedicated to preparing women for full citizenship rights and educating the country about issues at hand.[8] Like others in the room nodding enthusiastic assent, Catt saw the League as a potent political player addressing great democratic opportunity, in which women's nonpartisanship by virtue of previous exclusion would help sweep away "bad political habits," reinvigorating an improved electorate through the League's future civic education campaigns.[9]

There was widespread euphoria in the immediate aftermath of the Nineteenth Amendment's passage, as supporters projected a transformation in national civic character. Predictions were made that the country could now share in the suffragists' sense that a "common good" might be advanced through significant political reform and social progress made possible by the new female voting public. Jane Addams — affiliated with Hull House, pacifist work, NAWSA and unions — was an inspiring living example of the Progressive influences that dominated both this aspect of the suffrage movement and the ambitious post-1920 legislative agendas. Serving as adviser to the new League of Women Voters, she foresaw the political dimension of the nascent social reform movement as she pushed for rapid implementation of child labor laws, greater hygiene facilities, housing safety and concern for the "community."[10]

A Tough Beginning

The initial euphoria would disappear within months, causing a partial dissipation in legislative progress. Lynn Dumenil argues that the downswing was inevitable.

> Before national suffrage was achieved, a great many women — equally excluded from this basic right of citizenship — could come under the same umbrella of 'votes for women.' Once the Nineteenth Amendment was ratified, the lines that divided women — class, race, ideology — became more significant. By gaining the individual right they had so vigorously sought, they laid the groundwork for the fracturing of female community.[11]

As women suffragettes left behind their exalted social movement status in 1920 to evolve into more standard political players, their powerful bridging alliance would begin to fracture, not to coalesce again until 1972.

Upon its official launch on February 20, 1920, the League of Women Voters faced immediate challenges to its ability to "finish the fight" intact. Its most immediate assignment would be preparing women for their first countrywide presidential vote, months away. Most women were clueless how to pull the voting lever, let alone consider criteria for electoral choice, and the new League would help educate them for the task. Having ceded the presidency to Maud Wood Park, honorary president Carrie Chapman Catt urged women to take advantage of the historic moment:

> "The vote is a power, a weapon of offense and defense . . . . Use it intelligently, conscientiously, prayerfully. No soldier in the suffrage army has labored and suffered to get a 'place' for you. Their motive has been that women would aim higher than their own selfish ambitions, that they would serve the common good."[12]

In November 1920, failure came on a massive scale, with national voting turnout hitting an historic low. Some men argued that women generally and the League in particular had failed the country and their own membership with women's low electoral turnout. The primary tragedy came from inflated expectations of the League's capability to activate the newly enfranchised population, combined with widespread apathy on the part of both men and women. But it has proved historically inaccurate to exclusively blame women for either the 1920 election's low turnout or suggested female "docility" in what was for many women their first major election. Several scholars note the absence of national quantitative data separating the 1920 vote by gender, observing considerable variation by region, population density and ethnicity in terms of women's votes on record. Their findings challenge the common assumptions of the 1920s that women as a group failed to show independence or interest, though apathy was undeniably in the national mix. League Chronicler Louise Young concludes that it would take years of historical analysis to appreciate "the complexity of the psycho-cultural process required to make political participation a meaningful engagement for so severely subordinated a class… [The new political right had to become] merely a political instrumentality."[13]

The League of Women Voters also came under early criticism for its projected nonpartisan stance from established politicians from both the Democratic and Republican parties, concerned such independence masked a female challenge to their party primacy. As an example, when the League was formed in 1920, the governor of New York had chided them publicly for being, in his view, a female block organization, arguing forcefully that they must integrate into existing party organizations.[14] Suffrage activists like Alice Paul, who had advocated gender-block voting in 1920 to achieve an Equal Rights Amendment on the Nineteenth Amendment's surging tide (and would continue in that position until her death in 1977), were also disparaging. The NWP urged women to be single-issue voters for the ERA, a position the League rejected. The League's *Woman Citizen* took issue with Paul, titling its editorial "No Sex Line Up." The *Citizen* argued presciently that women would not vote for gender per se but rather would choose by class and personal interests. Carrie Chapman Catt and Maud Wood Park sought long-range maturation of the new voting population, improving the *competence* of women to take on the new duties of citizenship *irrespective* of the parties they chose to support and officially maintaining nonpartisan position toward specific candidacies. Sara Alpern and Dale Baum assert that the League contributed to post-1920 frustration of the women's movement through "opt[ing] for assimilation in the naïve hope of becoming men's equals overnight."[15] It could be argued that Presidents Warren G. Harding and Calvin Coolidge's elections, which unleashed administrations that disabled Progressive aims cherished by League members, drew in part from the League's restraint from drawing partisan lines in post-war sands.

Initial membership figures for the League of Women Voters also proved disappointing. Perhaps because of the new flapper era, the League's expectations for sustaining widespread intense engagement (common in the suffrage fight) produced fewer than 100,000 of NAWSA's previous millions as active members.[16] These figures could understandably be interpreted as a personal affront to long-striving suffragists, granted upon their victory a contracting, distracted audience. While Maud Wood Park hoped for the League to be an "every woman's organization," it quickly became apparent that those women rising through the League's ranks during the 1920s would be a special breed, distinct from the greater numbers choosing more standard women's clubs in full association vibrancy. As League archivist Barbara Stuhler notes,

> Not all suffrage women joined the League. Some simply drifted away and some younger suffragists found the new behavioral freedoms of the 1920s an enticing distraction. Other women followed their reform-minded inclinations into organizations focused on education, world peace, and other interests... If there was one development that characterized the post-suffragist era, it proved to be the myriad opportunities for participation of women volunteers in a host of associations reflecting a wide range of programs and projects. *The age of the woman as volunteer was about to come into full flower.*[17]

While some women undeniably preferred the more intoxicating version of clubbing in the early 1920s, it was becoming increasingly clear to many of their gender, made civic by hard experience, that a fight remained to make the vote uniformly real for all American women and men. There was a blizzard of anti-female voter activity across the United States throughout the 1920s, rationalized by both women and men as preserving women's good character by keeping them away from the polls. Low voter turnout in 1920 was at least partly due to institutional and behavioral obstructions by party officials, local judges and private citizens, who often stood to gain by preserving political bosses' power and minimizing unpredictable voters. Those most durably obstructed were lower-class women and men, who were ill-equipped to challenge the frequently arbitrary, threatening and confusing interventions. To complicate the issue, there was — and remains — considerable variation in voting ordinance and practice from state to state. Partial uniformity in national voting jurisprudence — or even the exercise of simple duties like jury calls — would await the early 1960s' federal empowerment legislation to enforce and regulate civic participation laws.[18]

Carrie Chapman Catt had initially guessed that the League of Women Voters' work to launch women into political life could be completed within five years, but this projection proved vastly premature.[19] League volunteer lobbyists, schooled from their long efforts to win suffrage one Congressman at a time, observed that government and political party advocacy was clearly lacking for those voters who were most vulnerable to arbitrary or deliberate exclusion, concluding that the League would need to help defend the new vote. Fortunately, these activists could learn from states like California and Oregon, which had offered women the vote in 1911 and 1912 respectively; over time, women residents in both places had learned how to counter obstructive tactics with grassroots preparation and legal challenges. A highly effective additional counter to obstruction came through shaming publicity, circulated nationwide by the League's *The Woman Citizen*.

The new association proved to be less prepared for the reactionary ferocity of the 1920s amidst the new "Red Scare" issuing from American reaction to Bolshevik victory in Russia. The War Department had secretly placed many suffragist groups under surveillance during World War One because of their championing of pacifism, negotiation, disarmament, and American participation in international organizations. In 1924 a "Spider Web Chart" circu-

lated among conservative publications and Congressional committees charging that the League of Women Voters and other women's
groups aimed to "disarm America."[20] The Spider Web Chart had
first been published in Henry Ford's *Dearborn Independent* in 1924,
but had originated in the Chemical Warfare Bureau of the War Department during World War One. The Daughters of the American
Revolution and other conservative groups repeatedly targeted "im-
plicated" groups like the League, another suspect being Jane Addams' Women's International League for Peace and Freedom. (Addams would subsequently win the Nobel Peace Prize for her work
within the latter in 1931.) To counter national isolationist sentiment
and unjustified vitriolic censure, the League responded energetically in *The Woman Citizen* to explain members' pro-democratic
positions. The Red Scare controversy gradually wound down, but
not before it had fundamentally damaged American women's reforming potential during their first political decade. The 1920s were
proving to be a confrontational period for the League and other
civic groups. League chronicler Louise Young would later dryly
note that social justice hadn't been "in season."[21] Nor would it be
later, when Senator Joseph McCarthy would resurrect the Spider
Web Chart as an example of subversive influences resident within
women's civic groups.

A Structural Response

The first several League presidents responded to these travails by
focusing on an internal structure that would enable the League of
Women Voters to survive the monsoon. Carrie Chapman Catt's visionary modeling of NAWSA to match federal government structure transferred to the new League as it capitalized on existing suffrage branches throughout American communities.[22] But the National League of Women Voters (thus named until restructuring
in 1944) was to be a confederated council of state leagues, banded
together at their discretion, until authority could be exerted on
feisty state chapters already buoyed in organization and funding
from hard-won suffrage battles. When issues of payment for the
new League arose, equity was impractical, since more pliant chapters were insolvent. Moreover, those few with funds wanted to as-

sert themselves on the policy committees, to national office dismay. The League's first convention produced, in president Maud Wood Park's words, a "kettle of eels" through undisciplined, personalized introduction of sixty-nine policy goals directly from the convention floor.[23]

While authority was gradually asserted within the 1920s by League presidents Park and Belle Sherwin to develop rational operation, it was rapidly clear that structural matters were of deep importance to widespread members and that fights on these questions would be personal and fierce. In an historical profile of League member motivation, James G. Hougland and James R. Wood observed that while many associations had passive members accepting hierarchical instruction, the League of Women Voters had been an exception from its start. Members objected to bossy behavior and cared *who* got association power. One reason was that "the goals of the League are likely to make democratic ideology particularly salient to members, thereby increasing the rewards of exercising control."[24] Throughout much of its history, League members have been "prominent" socially, expecting to be respected, heard and accorded standing. As a result of these combined factors, League history is dotted with control struggles judged worth winning.

From 1921-1923, the bulk of powerful state chapters of the League of Women Voters resisted central direction. Pennsylvania — destined to be a frequent annoyance — seceded from the national council and went its own way. Connecticut, Illinois, Indiana, New Jersey and New York also tended to be self-directed. Within Eleanor Roosevelt's New York state chapter in 1923, a power fight quickly emerged between the local New York City league and the state level. When the state leadership revised their constitution in favor of controlling city chapter funds, city members left, enraged.[25] Completely reliant on volunteer efforts, impeded in regularizing state incorporation, unable to collect dues from those carrying its name, and addressing a rowdy, shrinking membership, the League's national organization risked implosion.

In response to these difficulties encountered by the League of Women Voters during its first two decades, its structure took an abrupt turn toward both centralized operation and localized authority in 1944. With assertive action at the highest level through president Marguerite Wells, what most League historians term a legitimate "member revolt" against "non-responsive central [state] leadership" withdrew state charters and refashioned the association as the presently-termed League of Women Voters of the United States. Percy Maxim Lee, president in the 1950s, later judged that "the Membership itself determined what the League would be."[26] Henceforth, there would be three tiers — an elected volunteer president, a mix of appointed and elected boards of directors, and finally, local members, judged to be the core of the organization. Pledging dedication to grassroots engagement at the 1946 relaunch, new president Anna Lord Strauss would urge members to accept more responsibility for all tasks. (Strauss was also notable to civically-concerned women as the great-grand-daughter of Lucretia Mott, the Quaker abolitionist and advocate for women's rights who, together with Elizabeth Cady Stanton, authored and delivered the hallowed Declaration of Sentiments in 1848 to their assembled Seneca Falls Convention to launch the American women's suffrage movement.) League members responded exuberantly to Strauss' challenge, deluging Congressional offices on behalf of unified goals and bringing the League to new membership life. 1950s president Lee mused decades later that the shift to a League of individual members had saved the League from dissolution. The re-born association almost doubled its membership from 65,000 in 1945 to 125,000 in 1954, in apparent affirmation of the restructuring.[27]

An additional structural shift came in 1954. Indicative of changing fortunes, the 1950s had produced a proactive national office of the League of Women Voters of the United States with thirty-nine paid employees. (All officers would continue to be elected volunteers.) The League was and is technically a nonprofit 501c4 organization, tax-exempt but not tax-deductible due to its advocacy role. But negotiation of Cold War constraints caused its leaders to seclude the advocacy operations of the organization to facilitate greater independence for an educative branch. Thus in 1957 the League of Women Voters Education Fund was created as a 501c3 organization inviting tax-deductible contributions in support of "citizen education and research" to compliment the advocacy and political engagement of its sister organization yet maintain separate account.[28]

As of 2012, the two League of Women Voters organizations share the same board of trustees, staff and physical space, examples of the grey divisions among contemporary nonprofit organizations. League operation in both branches continues to be highly structured. All qualifying local Leagues are required to have by-laws consistent with the national office; to stay nonpartisan; to hold annual membership and regular board meetings; to pay a specified portion of membership dues to the state and national levels and have a local solvency plan; to strategize on diverse membership growth and retention; and to act organizationally and individually consistent with League principles. Uniform image is required, though forms of meeting are getting less stringent in a virtual era.[29]

Finding Purpose

The League's goals have exhibited remarkable constancy over time. A recent mission statement could have been written in 1920:

> The League of Women Voters, a nonpartisan, political organization, encourages the informed and active participation of citizens in government, works to increase understanding of major public policy issues, and influences public policy through education and advocacy.[30]

Yet within these lines, there are influences and target-audiences that clarify just what this civic association has been trying to achieve over the past century.

First, Quaker and Progressive values of social justice, development through education, consensual deliberation, and "missionary zeal for public service," are intrinsic to its goals, allure and operation, reflecting continuity with its roots. Contemplative individualist religious influence had been profound for the abolition, suffrage and progressive movements that made women political in the Nineteenth and early Twentieth Centuries, providing the conviction and faith that helped enable the winning of votes for women. (Lucretia Mott was a Unitarian minister; Susan B. Anthony was a Quaker; Jane Addams was raised Quaker though she became Presbyterian; Alice Paul was a Quaker. Many of the rank-and-file would draw from these church groups.) Daughters raised in the same spirit frequently became active in the League of Women Voters, continuing the missionary legacy.[31]

As the League of Women Voters convened for the first time in 1920, members adopted the 1912 Progressive Party platform as their own. Already receding in political power, the Progressive Movement's persuasive methodology, developmental social goals, and optimistic search for a generalized good would be durably preserved within the League and other public interest groups derived from the period.[32] To enhance deliberation, the League would be distinctive in a partisan-charged era by resolving to stay objective and independent while considering issues, educating its ranks on radical issues without necessarily taking an association stand on them.

Ninety-two years later, the League's Progressive platform has proved to have purposive backbone in it, not just operational style. Through active, even valiant advocacy, it would help transform what had previously been considered women's "dominion of reform" into the social welfare agenda of future generations, targeting industrial working conditions, child and maternal health improvements, fair wages, housing standards, expanded legal rights, and the pursuit of world peace. (Birth control would make an early priority list, though it became too contentious by the mid 1920s and was dropped from official consideration.)[33] Notable lobbying successes lay ahead, such as the passage of the landmark Sheppard-Towner Act of 1921, which increased hygiene education for infant and maternity care and inspired future New Deal welfare policy. (The League's partner in this effort would be the otherwise conservative General Federation of Women's Clubs. The program would exist with federal support until the Great Depression, when funding was allowed to lapse.)[34]

With the 1933 beginning of President Franklin Delano Roosevelt's four progressively expansive terms in the White House, the League of Women Voters would augment its influence over federal policy, witnessing the return to public popularity of the original 1912 Progressive Party platform. Most of those Progressive elements (described in Chapter 2) would become national policy in only slightly modified form by 1945 in spite of the 1920s' cautious delay, a remarkable lobbying achievement testimony to the merits of the long historical view.[35] It is no accident that these achievements coincided with Eleanor Roosevelt, stalwart League member since inception, using her position as First Lady to celebrate the League's tradition of developmental citizenship through nonpartisan association work. In gratitude, Eleanor Roosevelt's championing of the United Nations during the 1940s would produce the League's most massive public relations campaign of its long history, deluging feeble arguments to the contrary in governmental offices throughout the nation.[36]

An additional and consistent purpose of the League of Women Voters has been enabling the practical enhancement of American citizens through association engagement, bridging women's public and the private lives along the way.[37] Founding leaders had a firm faith in women's developmental capacity, particularly on the cusp of a yet-unsullied political judgment in 1920. During that period, women were culturally expected to exhibit special ability for moral judgment that might help them engage responsibly in the democratic process.[38] From the start, League identity as an "every woman's association" was sought in order to convert "average" women to rational discourse and energetic citizenship. But League leaders and members have been anything but average. By virtue of its members' accomplishments, origins and attitudes, the League's chapters have been vulnerable to charges of elitism and white middle-class bias in spite of stated aim to represent a "public interest."

In complement to Sidney Verba's eventual democratic theory focus on those who *do* participate in civic life rather than the characteristics of those who stay away, League leaders in the 1920s saw their best promise in representing *organized* women.[39] Particularly through the 1950s, the durably limited membership has been a cadre of "the most active, ambitious and politicized of the younger generation."[40] In some cases, members were transformed in this direction from previous political passivity or ignorance through communal engagement. Today, faith in the League's ability to improve voter judgment through the provision of solidly researched and debated information remains officially in place, though evidence of public opinion manipulation is not disregarded, a measure of the stubborn optimism and longevity required for the project.[41]

An additional enduring goal of the League of Women Voters has been the improvement, as opposed to the radical replacement, of democratic institutions, reflecting Progressives' faith in democratic government to address public problems. In practice, this has translated to literal League partnership with civil servants on particular projects, and there is some substance to the "establishment" angle of the League's history — including the final months before the passage of the Nineteenth Amendment, to National Women's Party chagrin — as a traditional "front door lobby."[42] This approach has not gone unrewarded. For example, in between 1970 and 1990, a number of past League presidents have ended up working for the White House at an assistant cabinet secretary level.[43] At the same time, elements of the League's critical social movement origins remain through its readiness to publicly reject the representational status quo and to politicize the American public toward change. In particular, League protests have emphasized the need for legitimacy, accountability and citizen responsibility. These may not be popularized subjects in the mass protest zone, but they are at the heart of responsible democratic governance.

While the League of Women Voters has always rejected partisan support of candidates, it has also made partisan *position* preferences clear from its inception. An important example of this fine line is its official support for the viability of female candidates *in general* as agents for advancing progressive social change. Seven women were elected to the U.S. Congress by 1928, with bigger gains at the state level. By 1929, almost 150 women served state and local governments. There would be disagreement during this period between the National Women's Party and the League on whom could be credited with the victories, but both celebrated the milestone for women's political progress.[44]

The League has also refused to settle for reenactments of 1920 and 1924's low voter turnouts, finding inspirational associational purpose to launch mass media campaigns and civic classes that shifted political culture toward grassroots outreach and institutionalized new relationships between citizen groups and politics. The League's "Get Out The Vote" drive had a huge effect on 1920s and 1930s political culture, if not yet in the actual numbers of people voting. The League could claim considerable credit for the formation of 3,000 "Get Out the Vote" groups in 46 states in between 1923 and 1928 that focused on publicizing voting rights and providing education on the particular elections. Liette Patricia Gidlow has argued that this trendsetting and effective association-led activity set in place a new relationship between citizen groups and politics.[45] It would become clear to League members that personal motivations to vote could be extremely powerful, and that the League could expand membership *and* increase turnout through finding connections between people's private experience and public affairs.[46]

The Importance of Style

Historians are increasingly aware that style can lend critical vigor or malaise to membership associations, calling for exploration of these deliberate choices to comprehend such organizations' allure and impact. Seemingly conciliatory and tame compared to women selecting more radical groups like the National Women's Party and the National Organization for Women, members of the League of Women Voters exhibited certitude from the start that both inward respectability *and* outward respect would best suit the achievement of their organizational goals. Respectability and decorum can be two-edged swords. Lynn Dumenil has contended that organizational selection of style was critical to the historical success of the women's suffrage movement via NAWSA's mass scale popular persuasion. She judges that organizational style likewise crippled political efficacy for newly enfranchised women in 1920 because of the influential League's assumption of nonpartisan objectivity at a moment of political opportunity.[47] On the other hand, such stylistic forbearance and objectivity would prove vital to the League's impressive persuasion of cautious Americans in the nearly successful Equal Rights Amendment campaign of the 1970s.

While drawing from exceedingly earnest forbears within egalitarian social movements, the League of Women Voters' style is more pragmatic, pursuing otherwise quixotic dreams through astute political organizing.[48] Its nonpartisan style is prone to public misunderstanding, since it may imply objectivity but also presents savvy long-term strategy. Partisan alliance can backfire. The classic example is when prominent NAWSA members supported ex-

President Theodore Roosevelt, the single pro-suffrage candidate, in 1912. When Roosevelt failed to win the Republican nomination for president or, as a Progressive, the general election, it would take eight more years and considerable courting of a harried and resentful President Woodrow Wilson for the suffrage groups to win the vote.[49] League members have found their best nonpartisan lobbying tools to be deep knowledge of democratic institutions and issues, paired with consistent display of the scruples for which they're known.

These exacting standards appear exemplary and do produce public praise, but they can also frustrate and disable the League of Women Voters among people playing by different rules. As an early example, Carrie Chapman Catt had learned from forty years of suffrage campaigning that "a minute minority of well-placed political leaders could frustrate an overwhelming preponderance of informed opinion," referring to Elihu Root, President Wilson's Secretary of State and earlier the bane of NAWSA's existence.[50] League strategists engaged in battles for the Equal Rights Amendment later recalled how they were patronized and ridiculed when lobbying for women's rights, then welcomed with praise when returning to the same offices on behalf of safer topics, concluding that they had been used, lied to, defied and, on that occasion, outmaneuvered.[51] But time and again, politicians have underestimated the League's endurance and reputable force. A 1954 observer captured the steely resolve behind polite demeanor of those who volunteer for the League experience:

> "Even when they are sneered at as a bunch of ladies' sewing societies, the League of Women Voters takes no offense. They just keep on needling politicians, influencing history, fighting the things they fear: dishonesty and bad faith."[52]

Like those from other associations and the social movements that can drive them, League members have managed personal and organizational adversity through friendship, shared values and pooled resources. With funding perennially scant, meeting style can be minimalist, but it is always social. Whether its functions feature the "tea" so popular through the 1950s or the "green bag" increasingly appearing on contemporary calendars, both invitations are welcomed and enjoyed in the social spirit of the work ethic and principles members embrace and the paltry sums available for their completion.[53]

While women's clubs are no longer fashionable, recent scholars have rediscovered their profoundly empowering role in helping otherwise disadvantaged women bond and develop together in "safe haven" to improve shared condition. Karen J. Blair judges,

> From clubs, seemingly tame in contrast to more militant types of activism, are created women leaders for positions of influence... Moderate behavior can deceive outsiders, who might cling to suspicion that women's groups cannot incubate meaningful changes.[54]

The public face of feminism can be misleading. Stolid appearing League members have built an impressive feminist record of legislative success and transformation of public opinion.[55] As Blair powerfully observes, "Far from peripheral to the boisterous women's rights advocates of the era, the League... cloaked its rebels... to be a congenial forum for change."[56] While more contentious feminists would dismissively underestimate League potential, considerable history supports the verdict that quiet, polite activists can be more effective than flamboyant ones.

One example of the effectiveness allowed by cloaked style is the League of Women Voters' highly effective campaign on behalf of women's rights in the 1960s and 1970s in southern states such as North Carolina. The difficult effort was made publicly non-threatening through lodging in familiar, stodgy, and most importantly, local vehicles like the League and the Young Women's Christian Association. Melissa Estes Blair's research has observed, "League of Women Voters women saw their letters and lobbying efforts [there] as countering both the outsider agitator image of the National Organization for Women and the emotional appeals of organized anti-ERA women."[57] Yet these two seemingly incompatible League and NOW styles, drawing from generational divide and preferred voice, would accommodate a purpose-driven national coalition that narrowly missed significant victory for the Equal

Rights Amendment. The two very different feminist organizations continue to work together on specific issues.

The League of Women Voters conscientiously steers its public voice toward middle ground in the national policy conversation. Percy Maxim Lee presided as president during the League's lagging efforts to racially integrate its internal operations in the 1950s. She rationalized avoidance of inviting blacks to join by noting, "The League cannot be a law onto itself . . . . It must not run too fast for its contemporaries of the American electorate to keep up . . . . It must in other words want the things that other *reasonable* American citizens want,"[58] edging a maximum diversity toward progressive goals. Though difficult to assess this position positively by contemporary values, Lee's civil rights strategy was not unusual for the time, positioning the League in what she perceived to be the mainstream, perhaps in the hope that it could thereby progress the nation's attitudes gradually and with less opposition.[59]

This rare misstep in the League of Women Voters' otherwise "politically correct" progressive positions drew in part from what Lee saw to be a practical recruitment issue. Through most of its history, the association has made deliberate efforts to avoid alienating mainstream voters (or, even worse, members) to expand potential impact. A contemporary journalist of Lee's recorded his understanding that it was these mainstream voters Lee hoped would respond to the League's voter education efforts in the 1950s and present themselves at the polls.[60]

On rare occasions such as the early Civil Rights era, the National office has indeed exhibited conservative, hesitant tendencies in comparison to local League activists, who in private have challenged national policies on matters like civil rights and the ERA.[61] But while some advocates term the League as staid and conservative, the charge is generally not appropriate except in relation to the national leadership's racial blinds prior to the 1960s. Mainstream may be the style, but historically it has not been the goal, since the League has both supported and eventually transcended the 1912 and 1924 Progressive Party platforms' visionary — if white-inclined — range.[62]

The League of Women Voters as an organization has become adept at surviving adversity. Linda Damaris Sayre has challenged

Lynn Dumenil's criticism of the League's nonpartisan determination in 1920, arguing that the early move saved the women's movement from being imprisoned within party bureaucracy. She also points out that the League has shifted from emphasizing its educative role in conservative eras to asserting advocacy in times of greater progressive promise, helping it survive to meet the needs of future generations officially unchanged despite its generally recognized liberal leanings.[63] This tightrope maneuver has not been easy. Loyal members have repeatedly been "bewitched, bothered, and bewildered" that the public is private-focused in spite of their best efforts, that citizens have frequently chosen not to learn about the issues, and that they have ignored energetic League reminders to show at the polls on voting day. [64] Leaguers have learned to steel themselves to defeat or under-appreciation of particular efforts, protecting resolve to continue education and advocacy efforts in the hope *next* time would be different. That "the next time" has presented itself for more than ninety-two years is testimony to canny weathering of volatile political developments.

Developing Through Process

When the League of Women Voters' state chapters were fighting for their particular "kettle of [policy] eels" in the 1920s, they were essentially scrapping over means versus ends as drivers of the League's future. These discordant reformers were in good contemporary company, as the country weighed efficient government through technocrats versus populist mayhem through class-surging democracy. The League's identity would crystallize and calm as Belle Sherwin, elected president in 1924, realized that *the association's means could be the end itself* through a focus on developmental process. New women voters needed information for "improved" judgment and engagement. While League leaders were confident such guidance should come from their offices, questions remained on its form and content. Moreover, frenetic League members seemed to need a focus that would inspire both personal and organizational longevity. Looking beyond the fray, Sherwin's epiphany was that "the [agenda] program is the thing," made legitimate through its evolution from local members and unifying through the consensual process of its formation.[65] Subsequent president Anna Lord Strauss noted that through the related undertaking of copious civic manuals (that continue to be the association's trademark product), League identity would further derive from the shared function and purpose of its members. The League chapters' educational focus would thereby enable connection with each member, potentially surpassing the value of the information itself through activating individual personal inquiry and loyal participation.[66] These manuals, in turn, would bridge the gap with members of the public, who purchased League materials and attended symposiums with increasing frequency. Through the following decades, League members would take great pride and ownership in their association's materials and proceedings, judging them of sufficient external as well as internal importance to justify careful cataloguing. By 1950, the League would successfully offer the largest single non-governmental-organization paper acquisition to the U.S. Library of Congress: 277 separate collections of League correspondence, meetings, reports, articles, and audio materials. The unusual extent of this public collection is, according to Louise Young (a LOC archivist as well as a chronicler of League history), testimony to the objective historical value accorded their proceedings.[67]

The year of that archive transferal coincided with the maturation of the League's vaunted grass-roots process that makes it such an outstanding example of a democratically beneficial civic association. The localized manner of internal decision-making was designed to "give the training — challenging in itself — to fit the citizen to serve" in the public interest through painstaking deliberative exploration within the local Leagues and subsequent national negotiation among positions to produce unified programs.[68] The basic League concept of "study – member agreement – action" would apply to how meetings were run, agendas were reached, debates were handled, and public meetings and materials were handled.[69]

Grassroots consensual process has proved to be a key element of that programmatic equation. Linda Damaris Sayre notes its distinctive evolution from suffragist Quaker influences.

Consensus does not mean that every member has to agree with every action or conclusion of discussions. It means everyone has a chance to speak if she or he chooses to and [that] those of opposing opinion to the general view feel they have their day in court even if the final consensus differs from their view. It is not a vote but a sense that there is *general agreement* and that there is a willingness to accept . . . the sense of the group . . . . It ideally involves a group process of learning, particularly learning to listen and respond to the opinions of others.[70]

Such valuation of equal opportunity for expression, listening and consideration on mutually fair terms is also integral to current modeling of deliberative democracy, which shares derivation from the Progressive thought which brought it to flower.[71]

Consensual process may flourish particularly well within the League of Women Voters at the local level, but it is also followed as an ideal for reaching national association positions as well. Debate is constantly underway at all levels to decide matters large or small. Stringent advocacy standards exist, and expressively motivated members take their responsibilities seriously to exhaustively consider all subjects in appropriate fashion before drawing conclusions. (These group probes constitute a significant joining motivation for most members.) Along the way, local Leagues and national staff undergo intense self-study to reconfigure methodology and interpersonal dynamic, yet another debate.[72] The League's commitment to methodical consensual process may by deliberative standards be admirable. As Progressive mentor John Dewey asserted in the 1920s and 1930s, the readiness to communally commit time, effort and resolving intent can unveil an advisable position as *"less a form of discovery than a form of association and communication in the solving of practical problems,"* discovering an approximation of the public interest along the way.[73] But this lauded process can also be "ponderous" and, to outsiders, interminable. Gloria Feldt, past-president of Planned Parenthood and ex- League member, has come to consider this process busy-work that misses the urgency of cause.[74]

There are practical limits to the League of Women Voters' consensual process. It must be funded at local chapter expense, affecting uniform depth. Generally viable at the local and state levels, consensus can be counterproductive or out of reach at biennial national conventions, where a degree of hierarchy reemerges. While policy-making officially draws from these conventions, the national League is directed on a daily basis by its volunteer board and a council featuring each state chapter. The best motivation within that setting to accurately represent local sentiment is peer approval.[75] Most likely, such feedback is generously available, in stark contrast to professionalized hierarchical associations dominant today.

League of Women Voters' materials note that "speaking with one voice" is important to effectiveness and unity at the National League level. State and local chapters are asked to restrain themselves from varying the official national positions once advocacy platforms are in motion for two-year periods.[76] More lobbying freedom comes to members *as individuals*; those acting on official League capacity require specific authorization and script and are literally on circumscribed time because of monitoring from the Internal Revenue Service. Current lobbying vehicles include the National Lobby Corps (started just prior to the revived push for an Equal Rights Amendment in 1971), which uses nominated Washington, DC-area members for practicality, though they receive briefing from the League's professional staff. In addition, an email alert system (termed the Grassroots Lobby Corps) provokes widespread national member advocacy on priority legislative issues. Finally, online advocacy tools are provided through all levels of League websites to educate and inspire spiraling individual activism on purposive issues.[77]

There are limits to the League's consensual quality when issues get really thorny. Some analysts question the League's ability to produce substantive decisions that are truly representative of either the diversity of its membership or a rigorously intellectual "public interest," suggesting most critically that the elaborate process doesn't produce viable *political* choices because of its slowness. In the midst of the 1950s Civil Rights crisis, it took years for the League to arrive at a responsive policy position, compromising its nonpartisan position through selective inaction. But once the consensual wheel does lodge in gear, its deeply committed outcome can drive a uniquely powerful lobbying force, for example in the push for a United Nations at the close of World War Two.[78]

Who Wants to Join

Joining motivations among League of Women Voters members are frequently earnestly purposive, social and — according to John Mark Hansen — "particularly sensitive to changes in income and fashion."[79] Hansen observes that League membership tends to increase by 5% in presidential election years, indicating heightened public awareness of the group's national voter education role as well as voters' national unease during the political cycle. Robert H. Salisbury has found that people have tended to sign up for the League when they are *concerned,* suggesting that the League's fortunes can thrive at points of societal trouble by tapping into citizens' expressive protection of particular threatened values through volunteer activism.[80] Hansen acknowledges the power of Salisbury's *expressive* participation analysis, indicating that the joining benefit for League members comes in the group's tested enabling of hands-on change, ready to make positive through additional labor and commitment a worried expression of society off-course.

Those generally white, educated and socially-prominent women who considered signing up from 1920 through the 1960s would observe that League of Women Voters volunteers were expected to plunge in with vigor and personal funds. The League in the first half of this period was frequently near bankruptcy, so subsidy from its offices to cover volunteer activities was unavailable. Its tendency to rely on members' personal funds predictably limited those who got involved to women with spare time and a measure of help at home.[81] Ethnic and class diversity was thereby less bridging that the good intentions brought to bear with the usually progressive personal views representing both established parties. But in compensation, League members observed exciting developmental opportunities for civic training and purposive chances to effect change in their local communities. As an example, a Voters Service launched by the League in 1924 trained its volunteers as impartial recorders of data on ballot issues, polling information and candidate profiles. For those who consulted — or prepared — the materials, the caliber of their democratic decisions improved.

Eleanor Roosevelt provides a well-known example of the small yet intense cadre of the League of Women Voters' early members. She first got involved in 1920 at a friend's suggestion, shyly inaugurating a public life that would begin tentatively on the League's New York Chapter Legislation Committee, then proceed to its New York Board of Directors in 1922 and bloom with her chairing of the National Platform Committee on Social Legislation in 1924. Roosevelt would then veer toward the national Democratic Party's committee structure in 1928 while maintaining active League membership in a non-leadership capacity (befitting her increasingly partisan national position and in accordance with League rules), becoming supreme welfare lobbyist within her husband's four presidential terms. While in the White House, Roosevelt touted the League as a great source of nonpartisan information gathering and dispersal. She stayed faithful to the positions she had gained through League membership, and was particularly concerned about the need for ongoing voter education in a complex needs-pressed democracy. Like other League members, she preferred incremental change and chose to influence yet not impersonate women's improved status. But Roosevelt's restrained role did not limit the unique power of her gadfly progressive influence within her husband's terms in regard to civil rights, labor relations and a host of other causes. After Franklin Delano Roosevelt died in 1945, she was made the first United Nations Delegate representing the United States, to her former associational colleagues' thrill and durable energetic support.[82]

Gertrude Weil provides a slightly different version of an early League of Women Voters activist. First president of the nascent North Carolina chapter of the League in 1920 and daughter of German immigrants to the United States, she was concurrently active in the North Carolina Federation of Women's Clubs, the North Carolina Association of Jewish Women and other groups associated with women's and Jewish causes.[83] The League would prove an effective civic entry point for generations of immigrants to come.

A tangible sense of reforming purpose infused gradually multiplying League of Women Voters members during the Roosevelt administration. Genevieve B. Earl exemplified indomitable zeal, serving within the New Deal as private volunteer, social worker, Minority Leader of the New York City Council and head of Brooklyn's League Chapter. Reflecting the association's emerging emphasis on grassroots activism, Earl believed that engagement within urban administration efforts presented the great civic need of the time:

The fight for good government, while a winning one, is never permanently won. It must be waged afresh each day. To
keep eternally at this job is an act of faith and courage . . . .
[But] the job of being an alert citizen is exciting, relatively
easy and wholly rewarding.[84]

With the League of Women Voters' 1946 reorganization from a con-
federation of State Leagues to a grassroots, member-based national
organization, a doubling in size and stretching of diversity would
occur by 1955 as increasing numbers of American women responded to neighbors' calls for further-heightened engagement and responsibility through active League membership.[85] Accepting me-
nial along with lofty assignments, the reenergized group plunged
into the distribution of leaflets, circulation of petitions, and voter
registration drives that supplemented program meetings. While
failing to transform the League toward greater solvency, these
dedicated volunteers provided sufficient hours and dues to lift the
group's operations toward a new diversified level, in the process
giving them deep personal satisfaction from their connection with
what would prove to be its golden era.[86] Helen Gouldner examined
member commitment during the 1960s, the highpoint of League
membership, and found *very* high commitment to the League
across its membership, in direct correspondence to the degree of
volunteered labor. Long hours spent in preparatory research, plan-
ning meetings, negotiations toward consensus, and subsequent civic efforts gave solid testimony to herculean civic joiner tendencies
that would have amazed cynics like Mancur Olson. Officers tended
to effectively sign their lives over to the cause, slightly distrustful of
the "outsiders" who reserved the right to engage in other organizations as well. Those most vulnerable to leaving the association were
philosophically supportive but activity-wise distant.[87]

   Beginning in the mid-1950s, the League of Women Voters'
membership would be significantly impacted by the Civil Rights
and Women's Movements. But until 1970, the transformation
would lodge less in member profile change than in advocacy shifts
for the group and members' availability for traditional volunteer
functions. The League's wide structural reach within far-flung
communities preselected by degree those Americans who would

become active in the emerging social crusades of the time, enabling wider association-level engagement in these reforming movements than otherwise possible. As Melissa Estes Blair observes, "conducting feminist action *through existing groups* determined who would and would not participate in public feminist action in one Southern town."[88] The same point could be made about numerous other communities. Diversity came gradually to even the most staid Leagues. People with slightly different world-views had new motivation to join in the politicized protest era, contributing to 1969's surging League membership gains which produced an all-time high for their roster. Given the fact that many chapter-based membership federations dramatically lost membership during America's Civil and Women's Rights movements (from 1955 – 1995, the General Federation of Women's Clubs lost 83.1% in membership; the Masons lost 69.8%), *the League's relatively steady membership throughout those storms is testimony to its resilient reputation for moderate democratic engagement and social change.*[89]

The League of Women Voters would eventually be dramatically transformed by the shifting roles and opportunities for women during the 1960s and 1970s. While its members continued to largely be educated, suburban, white, middle-aged, married and hyper-committed in 1972, their roles as volunteers began to change in response to widespread female departure from home-life for competing demands from work, school and politics.[90] In a curious twist, League activists had been lauded for half a century for their efforts to empower women through volunteer association engagement, but they found themselves slammed fifty years later by the National Organization for Women for demeaning women through encouraging unpaid service.[91] In specific response to the societal evolution impacting most membership associations of the time, League tasks were combined and some responsibility was diluted; passive dues-paying members became officially acceptable.

Heading into a new era of heightened rights for women, the League of Women Voters tilted toward new life as a professional life enhancer to complement its civic purposes, carrying forward the traditional non-working volunteers as well, though in slightly muted form as their ages rose and numbers began to dwindle. Age frequently divided association choices at the point of the Equal

Rights Amendment's defeat in 1982, with 93% of League members topping 39 and 72% of those choosing the National Organization for Women dipping below 35.[92] Yet neither organization despaired of wider age participation; there was a general competition among feminist associations for members. John Mark Hansen later contended that the League won that competition, particularly for civic activists adverse to radicalism or stridency: "The League's decentralized, participatory character… made it better able to provide an important collective benefit" than some of those more traditionally hierarchical organizations less open to member engagement."[93]

By 2012, members of the League of Women Voters continue to attend meetings across the United States, contributing to a viable if waning participatory association presence in American civic life. Peter Levine observed in 1994 that "just 2.8% of the [U.S. population] said that they were members of some groups like the League of Women Voters, or some other group . . . interested in better government."[94] Characterization has shifted only slightly. Members continue to be well-educated, generally female (though men have been invited since 1974), middle-class, appreciative of citizen rights, and resolved for change. Many work or are retired. Eligible voting members must be citizens and at least 19 years old.[95] Recent webpage profiles include a former National Board president from Albuquerque, whose civic impulse as lawyer and federal civil servant led her to the League because of the Hatch Act; a Japanese-American, who resolved her World War Two detention experience through acknowledging the seriousness of League efforts to improve America; a recent immigrant to Delaware invited by one of her citizenship sponsors; an Oregon housewife whose research work for the League qualified her to work as a local investigative journalist; a young mother from Minnesota who joined to have meaningful social engagement despite attending to diapers; and an entrepreneur from California who found her League membership instrumental to a rise in city politics and black community activism.[96]

Those people who join the League of Women Voters expect to directly lobby Congress following careful study of the issues. As indication of their lobbying enthusiasm, the League and the Sierra Club both had their nonprofit status revoked because of excessive lobbying in the early 1970s. ("Substantial" was viewed at that time as anything more than 10%.) League members have since learned to be more protective of the League's 501c3 and 501c4 status in the delivery of the same function, also benefitting from the liberalization of nonprofit lobbying limitations to 20% in 1976. But while the League benefitted in theory from that expansion in lobbying potential, so did associations with greater financial resources and arguably fewer scruples.[97]

Members of the League of Women Voters are likely to be moderately progressive in their views, and are unlikely to attract conservatives to their consensual exploration.[98] Through the 1970s, the League originally featured a healthy balance of Republicans and Democrats in its membership. Louise Young records a comment of Maud Wood Park, the League's first president which is indicative of lasting orientation: "The League had chosen [in its first five years] to be a 'middle of the road' organization in which persons of widely different political views might work together [on] a program of definite advance... to lead many women a little way at a time." [99] But the increasing national polarization of conservative versus centric politics gives some credence to the possibility that most members presently vote Democratic or independent, and even that conservatives might feel socially ostracized as members. Linda Damaris Sayre comments, "this [liberal tendency] may affect the degree to which League consensus discussions really capture significantly dissenting viewpoints, as well as implications for possible selectivity of membership."[100] Some critics charge that this membership characteristic compromises the officially nonpartisan League stance, categorizing the League as a predictable liberal interest group. For example, the Foundation for Education Reform and Accountability (itself a lobbying group of conservative orientation) charged in February 2011 that the League of Women Voters New York was locally biased in favor of teachers' unions, with opposition to "school choice" and "property tax limits" the likely product of regular, "undisclosed" donations from the New York State United Teachers Union.[101]

Where the Numbers Go

In some ways, membership within the League of Women Voters has stayed frozen in time — until one recalls the relative growth in the American population and recent catapulting launch of particularized group millions.[102] Four years into the League's existence in 1924, membership had settled to 100,000, disappointing to Carrie Chapman Catt, who had hoped to sustain suffrage activism. Numbers dropped alarmingly with the Jazz Age and Great Depression, reaching 41,000 in 1934; the League was forced to rely almost entirely on volunteers and insist on localism because of national shortfalls. But those members like Eleanor Roosevelt who stayed were highly loyal, active and capable, compensating for sisters who abandoned progressive cause. With the launch of the New Deal, the fortunes of the League shifted. Surviving the restructuring toward local League membership that began in 1944, membership had returned to 62,000 by 1946. Rosters climbed to 93,000 by 1950, then 106,000 in 1952 and 125,000 in 1954, and both local Leagues and national profile spread throughout the country. Minneapolis itself had over *fifty-one* local leagues in 1954.[103] Through the Kennedy administration, joining figures reflected an elective enthusiasm toward energetic League engagement, *personally promoting democracy and the "free world" through civic values.* Barbara Stuhler considers 1950 to be the League's highpoint of visibility and respect. Shortly after that year, George Gallup would term the League "the greatest civic army of all time."[104]

Yet in this midcentury season of great public respect and visibility, the League of Women Voters' budget was extremely tight, operating with national budgets such as the miniscule $210,212 of fiscal year 1952-53. Drawing from local League tithes, national leaders felt the need to pinch both pencils and policy fights. As a result, president Percy Maxim Lee would choose to assume a low association profile in the 1950s in a period when other groups exhibited principled civil rights promise to avoid losing its members and funds. She drew a lesson from membership travails in the North Carolina State League, which had declined throughout the 1920s, reaching 100 people by 1931. Five years later it officially disbanded, reopening in 1951 at the behest of several women who considered the League the best available model for civic-inclined women. Seeking advice from Lee on how to address the question of race — highly relevant in North Carolina given its role within the lunch-counter sit-in movement then developing — the women were told to hedge black requests for membership and focus on retaining the state's still recovering white membership. The national League leadership resisted both taking a stand on civil rights and integrating its own ranks when the Supreme Court issued its Brown versus Board of Education decision in 1954. Rod Clare, who has studied this period of North Carolina history, finds the League's mid-century position tantalizingly disappointing in the context of both the state and the country at large.[105]

Yet it was the same President Lee who bravely risked official condemnation when she testified against Senator Joseph McCarthy in 1955. On that occasion, Lee stood her ground on behalf of civil liberties: "I believe tolerance and respect for the opinions of others is being jeopardized by men and women whose instincts are worthily patriotic, but whose minds are apparently unwilling to accept the necessity for dissent within a democracy."[106] With her support, the League of Women Voters had begun the 1950s with community education programs on civil liberties and federal loyalty policies, and officially advocated enhanced protection of individual rights. The inconsistent approach seemed to pay off in terms of national reputation, but did little to accelerate association growth. By 1962, Senator George Aiken, Republican of Vermont, would famously exclaim: "Only 135,000 of them? I thought there were millions!"[107]

In 1969, membership in the League of Women Voters reached an historic high, with 156,780 members and 1,300 local Leagues. But the period of growth was ending and membership began to decline at variable rates, causing League presidents to ponder unseemly recruitment and passive membership. Through the mid-1960s, leaders placed more importance on developing the League's famous program than in filling a room to consider it. But by 1980 one activist commented,

> We have engaged in too much self-flagellation during the last two years over the undeniable fact that women are going back to work and to schools in every increasing numbers. The trend has become part of our rationale for de-

creasing membership and recruitment difficulties. I do not
believe the volunteer is disappearing but that the *role of the
volunteer is changing significantly.*[108]

Such thinking proved partially deluded. A decade later, in spite of
a waxing Equal Rights Amendment campaign and unprecedented
fundraising, the League's membership had declined by 14% — not
as extreme as the General Federation of Women's Clubs' near-ex-
tinction during the period, but disquieting to exhausted members
nevertheless. Roberta Francis calculates that the League raised $2.5
million in all manner of ways to fund the ten-year ERA fight. But
the effort left the membership exhausted and frustrated.[109]

Yet while the League of Women Voters' numbers tilted south,
more radical feminist groups were not the ones to pick up the slack
in the materialist 1980s. While the National Organization of Wom-
en's membership shot up from slightly over 1,000 in 1970 to 35,000
in 1974 and 40,000 in the latter 1970s, its numbers had returned to
35,000 by 1980 in spite of the ERA ratification drive.[110] Numbers
for the League began to climb back in defiance of the earlier trend
(perhaps reflecting eventual concern with societal direction), and
returned by 2009 to 110,000 "members." Increasingly, the word
"member" is less associated with League strength than "supporter"
in recognition that checkbook participants are helping keep the association alive.[111] In 2011, the League claimed 140,000 "supporters"
and more than 800 Leagues in all 50 states.[112]

As a percentage of national population within the United
States, national numbers for the League of Women Voters have always remained small, constituting 0.00087% in 1924, descending to
0.00032% in 1935, bouncing back to 0.00077% in 1969, and returning to 0.00036% in 2005. But the *comparative resilience of the League's
membership relative to the General Federation of Women's Club's plunging decline* from 0.14021% in 1924 to 0.00032% in 2011 is striking in
its consistency. Curiously, *the League's national percentage trends are
quite similar to its ex-Spider Web enemy, the Daughters of the American
Revolution* (DAR), whose exclusive criteria and nativist advocacy
make it the antithesis of a bridging organization despite genetic affiliation with the nation's democratic past; DAR's members as a percentage of national population stayed just above the League's curve

from 1924 to the present (though missing the League's descent during the Depression years). Comparative materials on membership trends relative to national population for the League, the GFWC and DAR are presented in graphic form in Appendix 1 of this work, making clear the commonality in numbers with DAR and the difference from those of GFWC. More detailed graphic depiction of the League's membership trends relative to U.S. population totals is found in Appendix 2, indicating more clearly the League's varying fortunes over time.

In-house historians of the League of Women Voters continue to view their association as "the leading civic organization in the United States."[113] Its membership and staff have maneuvered the new digital age with relative dexterity. Practical steps have been taken to combine local Leagues, host virtual meetings, promote professional opportunities, and become flexible in a volunteer-disparaged world. The League's 2008-2009 annual report comments,

> While economic realities demanded that the League find new ways to communicate with members, train staff and carry out other essential activities in 2009, we saw this as an opportunity to adopt new technologies to complement and strengthen our work. From putting videos about judicial independence on YouTube to using Facebook as part of our advocacy in support of the League's position on health care reform, this year the League was on the cutting edge of online education and activism.[114]

A current League of Women Voters Membership Recruitment Initiative aims to draw "recently retired women aged 50-65, who are looking for civic engagement opportunities."[115] In the spirit of Kenneth T. Andrews and Marshall Ganz's advice to public interest associations recorded in Chapter 5, the League is training volunteer leaders of the future through the Ruth Shor Fellows program, established by bequest in 2009.[116] In spite of recent efforts to recruit minorities, the League has remained predominantly white. In 2002, 5% of League members were "of color," though the numbers would increase marginally in chapters containing greater geographic diversity.[117]

The League of Women Voters' political impact has spread beyond the suburbs with online posting of voter education, issue assessment and advocacy work that assist traditional efforts conducted in person. During electoral seasons, it increasingly allies with minority activation groups to increase their voter turnout. As an example, the League hosted "Beyond Election Day: Young People Getting Involved in Democracy" in Washington, DC on October 28, 2010, featuring presentations by the National Coalition on Black Civic Participation, the Pew Hispanic Center and the Student Association for Voter Empowerment. These sessions in theory level the political playing field; but they also conceivably solidify conservative readiness to obstruct the projects and reject League recruitment for their membership.

In the midst of membership constraints and internet-impacted reduction in publication sales, the national League of Women Voters' budget rose from $2.6 million during the 1990s to $6,560,476 in fiscal year 2007-2008.[118] This enlarged budget allows for greater programmatic impact on a national level, but it is also increasingly allocated to fundraising. Using fiscal year 2008-2009 as an example, fundraising represented 62% of supporting services and about 20% of total program expenditure.[119] Membership fees have stayed constant, in appreciation of members' frequently fixed incomes; officials continue to be volunteers and staff salaries are modest. The League's expanded national presence and budget are thus highly vulnerable to wobbling local League tithes, member donor fatigue and grant competition focused on the foundations known to support civic associations.

Potential civic grants at the national level for the League of Women Voters may come from the Pew Charitable Trusts, the Kettering Foundation, the Kaiser Family Foundation and the Joyce Foundation, all dedicated to developing and improving public dialogue, among other aims. But the League has uneven success winning their funds, in spite of its long record as a public interest group. Community foundations are more consistent prospects on local levels, but they tend to provide modest grants to the League that pale in comparison to the larger funds they bestow on particularized targets like *La Raza*. Corporate foundations can be more reliable funding sources for voter education efforts and issue studies. Advocacy fundraising provides yet another distinct group of funders, including groups like the Open Society Institute. The League has reasonable prospect for such funding, especially when allied with other "good government" groups like Common Cause and the Sunshine Project, but the products of the grants tend to be challenged immediately by well-funded groups on the other side of the ideological spectrum. Additional funds come as corporate matching gifts via employee designation and in-kind services provided by "affinity partners" for teleconferencing and internet technology in return for widened market exposure.[120] But even within the liberalized funding environment rendered by the "Citizens United" decision rendered by the Supreme Court in 2010, foundations are careful in their selection of civic education grantees; such activity can affect elections and, depending on the orientation of the courts, be charged with partisan effect.

Some of the most needy competition comes from the League of Women Voters' own ranks. Local Leagues are required to ask permission of state Leagues (who in turn must ask the national office on their own behalf) regarding approaches to foundations or corporations whose boundaries extend beyond the local jurisdiction.[121] Several chapters have impressive revenue and reserves, such as "Centre County's" $2,533,086 and $4,123,887 respectively for 2009, but others are unprepared for recession shortfall, like "Jefferson County" with yearly revenue of $20,429 and depleted reserves.[122] The League of Women Voters of Washington, DC had a comparatively healthy budget of $38,580 for fiscal year 2011, though it projected a need to draw $8,000 from reserves in anticipation of dues and donation shortfalls.[123] *These uneven financial numbers combine with decreasing membership to reduce the total national number of local Leagues. In 1969, there were 1,300 chapters of the League of Women Voters. By 2008, the number had shifted to 850, and by 2011 there were 800.* As a consequence, meetings continue to focus on civic concerns but with a survival edge that suggests vulnerable awareness of aging League communities.[123]

In spite of the League of Women Voters' "most valuable asset" — its dedicated members, whose generous volunteering efforts have conferred "clout, visibility and credibility" to the League for ninety-two years — its future is unlikely to become promising unless a stirring advocacy cause can be found, similar to the United Nations or the Equal Rights Amendment, that serves to diversify the age and derivative of its membership.[125] Chapter 7 will explore whether the dire condition of American democracy can produce such a cause, and to what extent the League's sustained efforts on its behalf may remain unsung.

7

Rendering "Congenial" Change on a Federated Scale:

Considering the League of Women Voters' Democratic Impact

Political experts frequently comment on a radical divide between how democracy should occur and what it presents in practice. But a wide range of theorists *and* practitioners of democratic process tend to set the League of Women Voters aside as an unusual exception to this rule, suggesting that its practical operation meets nearly ideal standards of assembled democratic citizenry and encourages improved governmental performance.[1] Why the League is accorded such respect, and whether its operations undermine elements of the reputation, provide the focus of this chapter.

Chapter 3 explored measures of a democratically beneficial public interest association. The standards appear unreasonably onerous by contemporary standards. Can a single civic association hope to provide active and personally meaningful membership that schools participants in practical democracy? Can it foster productive interpersonal dialogue among pluralistic cultures when its own environment is by degree a safe haven of commonality? While representing personally interpreted interest, can it help balance diffusively representative voices in national debates through honoring Constitutional process and abiding by Robert's Rules of Order? Can it defy the free rider odds and empower collective action on public problems? Can a utilization of internal democratic structure widen personal member effectiveness in a way that also empowers collective association voice?

Mark E. Warren has described ideal association-derived "dispositions that underwrite the democratic process," requiring good faith in deliberation and attending to a common good.[2] While according high marks to the League of Women Voters, he judges such "democratic associational ecology" a rarely achieved standard for American associations of either public or private orientation. If a jaundiced American population disparages its capacity to measure up in assembly to exacting democratic standards, its skepticism is — by contemporary example — understandable. Yet, in a manner the Banks children of Mary Poppins fame might have applauded, the perfect association governess is at hand, "practically perfect in every way.[3] The League of Women Voters will be found on examination to render acceptable to stellar performance on practically every measure of a democratically beneficial civic association. But can one association, even one such as the League, contribute within America to shared civic values among an oft-times disinterested, distrustful general population, loathe to accept tutorial intervention? To understand both the character of the League's near unique qualifications and the limits to their external and internal value in spite of theoretical approbation, it is helpful to plumb the League in greater operational depth.

In the process, an additional task will be examining how the League of Women Voters ranks on the combined democratic measures relative to the general association sector trends of professionalization, partisanship, passivity, inequality and exclusion described in Chapter 2. Evaluating the divide in such impact will clarify a range of League performance that reflects the extent of societal challenge more than a judgment of its internal failure. Yet resting on molding laurels will not help the League revive as either a grassroots membership organization or lonely herald of democratic engagement. Critical internal examination of its efforts to sustain a democratic record follow below on subjects as diverse as representing interest, playing by established rules, embracing difference, balancing ends versus means, and threading forward its gender-influenced advocacy in a supposedly post-feminist age.

Training for Democratic Engagement

The first democratic marker addresses whether membership within the League of Women Voters helps people experience pluralism. Warren has suggested that civic associations are less stratified in theory than those requiring particular qualifications for entry, thus containing bridging potential to enlarge democratic spirit.[4] But since it is elective, the League's membership has never been an accurate cross-section of American society. In general, the group has been durably white, middle-class, female, and reform-inclined, already disposed by degree toward civic life. (In fairness, the League has succeeded in activating some previously unengaged citizens, particularly during the 1950s and 1970s, through purposive idealism, social lures and training.) Increasingly, the League's membership features busy professionals, a decided change from past eras when volunteerism presented the principle civic path available to American women. Its strongest contemporary claim for asserting the experience of pluralism relates to its wide-ranging purposive agenda. As Sidney Verba has indicated, there are times when people of one class can develop a capacity to represent the interests of another.[5] Through past experience and present principle, League members increasingly address issues that pertain to a wide population, conscientiously balancing cross-class interests in presentation of policy options. Active League advocacy is often on behalf of disadvantaged populations, confounding outsiders' expectations of probable middle-class orientation given members' traditionally suburban origins.

The League of Women Voters cannot be termed a consistently transformative bridging vehicle in terms of its membership policies or rosters. Has the existence of durable niches and attitudes constrained its democratic impact in spite of purposive intent? Certainly it can be scrutinized on the basis of class origin. For example, Percy Maxim Lee, the League president who advised North Carolina members to delay their local Leagues' racial integration in the 1950s, presided manor-style over a personal Connecticut estate. Benefiting from her family's Maxim Gun Company, her domain featured horses and stables, children in boarding schools, a corporate executive husband, and Irish setters to complete the picture.[6] Given socially prominent leaders like Lee at various moments of the League's history, people with fewer resources might understandably elect for engagement in more socially reflective associations that arose, for example, with the rise of the urban community organization movement.[7] Through the 1950s, the League could also be challenged on its internal racial policies through passive lack of welcome for non-whites rather than formal exclusion. Colored Women Voters Leagues and the Colored Women Republican Club were among early separate deliberative vehicles encouraged by the League from 1920 through 1955 (see Cooney, *Winning the Vote*, 420).

The League of Women Voters' dragged response to pressures for racial integration was rejected by all levels of its membership in the 1960s without backward glance, and women such as Lee became white-gloved, if hardworking, rarities in recession-hit Connecticut. Over time, the League's national profile has expanded to include men and to feature gradually increasing ethnic diversity. As an example, League members elected Carolyn Jefferson Jenkins of Colorado in 1998 as the first black American to serve as League president; she is still active in her local chapter.[8] But national selection of black League leadership has not been repeated, and trends toward white dominance are stubborn. As of 2002, 5 percent of League members were "of color" in spite of an official association policy that encouraged racial diversity.[9] Currently the League's members are increasingly older than the rest of the American population, even if their attitudes and stamina are frequently youthful and in rejection of checkbook participation. With age and time constraints ineluctably narrowing a degree of membership, busy or impoverished people may choose an association more specific to their personal needs.

It is emphatically true that the League of Women Voters trains people for active democratic life. Mark E. Warren has observed that this particular association is well suited to induce real deliberation and engagement because its members buy into concepts of communal issue-resolution through active citizenship *before* they join. Warren calls such deliberate membership "cognitively defended commitment," with shared endeavors governed by principle rather than necessity.[10] The League's dedication to uncovering internal consensus is solution-directed rather than interest-bound. This method may be slow and seemingly lacking in drama, but its pace toward solid outcome is faster than most sessions of the United States Congress. Inward opinion formation at group sessions gives each person present a voice, in faith that the "sense of the group" will exhibit enlarged judgment. But League members have learned from their ultimately unsuccessful efforts to win national support for the Equal Rights Amendment within the 1970s. It is frequently wise to focus respectful education campaigns toward those who disagree rather than lingering with the supportive choir.[11] External opinion formation is therefore increasingly oriented toward non-members in the hope of shifting prospects for national deliberative debate.

It is also clear that the League of Women Voters empowers members as both association participants and enhanced individuals. As Sidney Verba, Kay Lehman Schlozman and Henry Brady have pointed out (see Chapter 4), joiners have a distinct advantage in democratic life, gaining inside knowledge of resources and players, reaching a wider audience with their views, and gaining the leadership skills in a friendly setting before unleashing them on less collegial turf. League members are on the inside track of public awareness, without record of seeking associated personal benefit. Linda Damaris Sayre has observed that many League members consider their League efforts to resemble a job — certainly volunteer time can equate to a part or full-time work schedule and may lead to official employment in other quarters — providing training in public speaking, media, written expression, advocacy, organization and tight budgeting.[12] Susan Hartman points out that the League has frequently acted as a sort of "farm club for women politicians," sourcing future leaders through providing training, information and solidarity as they prepare to enter the male-dominated political arena.[13] As a result, League membership for active citizens often transfers to their eventual candidacy for political office, and therefore cannot be underestimated for long-term political impact. Regardless whether they take this path, members grow interpersonally through mentoring, networking and befriending a modicum of internal diversity along the fringes of policy concerns.

It is useful to look at both the form and degree of members' commitment to the League of Women Voters to further understand the democratic value in their personal allegiance.[14] Their motivations have been found to be largely value-based, expressing through active membership a regard for issues, a literal embrace of democracy to enable their resolution, and a pursuit of Progressive goals that still bear resemblance to those heralded in 1912 and adopted by the League as guiding principles in 1920 (see Chapter 2 and 6). These are people who consider themselves more dedicated to public accountability and collective action than to preoccupation with private rights.[15] They exhibit extremely high association dedication because of these common values, deep personal bonds that develop in that appreciation, and a sense of enlarged efficacy.[16] The League's tangible membership incentives, presenting in the range of policy groups and voter guides, lack allure for those seeking more enticing direct compensation. For the distinctly small minority of Americans energized by the concept of democratic reform, such perks contribute toward filling a small, sometimes virtual room with open entry yet daunting residence. (Theoretically available exit can be complicated by guilt among intimate colleagues and friends.) The primary democratic asset in these attitudes is one of abiding social concern.

Just how durable is this motivation? John Mark Hansen has suggested that as "a consequence of its reliance on intangible incentives, League membership has been particularly sensitive to changes in income and fashion."[17] But cumulative membership data presented in Chapter 6 suggests that membership in the League of Women Voters is in fact fairly stable *relative to volatile patterns for other civic groups* such as the General Federation of Women's Clubs (see Chapter 2 and 6). Yet the League's democratic activation is not eternal, as its gradually declining numbers and folding local chapters show. Time, money and shifting priorities are impacting even the most dedicated of its contemporary members. With volunteers diminishing for *all* membership associations within the United States, the League will avoid dissolution or professionalization only if its declining grassroots trend is reversed.[18]

Experiencing Democratic Process

The degree to which associations are "incubators" of democratic political norms is seen most clearly in the structure and process that form their political voice.[19] When decision-making is inclusive and decisions evolve collectively from the grassroots level upward through the ranks, the association structure tends to be a federation of actively engaged volunteer members. Such is definitely the case for the League of Women Voters, a classic and time-tested example of federated structure. The fact that the League's democratic internal process is ongoing, open and consensual — underlining a shared faith that each individual will reason an optimal internal or external path through deliberating exhaustively with others — gives members a sense of inclusion and opportunity only partly deflated by human maneuvers. It is particularly beneficial that *all* members are welcomed to engage, multiplying the development effect and enriching the diversity of expressed views. The practice of retaining all officers as volunteers contributes to additional dedication not found in more hierarchical, professionalized associations.[20] The League's study groups troll wide-ranging opinion and data, contributing eventually to identification of mutually justifiable collective action, which in turn reeducates individual understanding and action. Externally, Leaguers urge all levels of government and community to partner in this topical exploration as a reliable means to address public concerns. Such operating principles, closely associated with the League throughout its history, align naturally with American democratic ideals of equality, self-rule, local direction and pursuit of public interest through process.[21]

Fostering Education That Spurs Civic Participation

Shifting to public awareness of what the League of Women Voters actually does, first on many people's lists will be the association's celebration of an activated American civic culture. But there will be considerable national disagreement on what such civics encompasses. Matt Leighninger, for example, notes that contemporary parlance of "civic" engagement encompasses "conflict resolution practitioners, deliberation experts, campaign finance reform advocates, democratic theorists, dialogue specialists, and representatives of many other related fields . . . [all with] divergent ideas about democracy and citizenship."[22] The League's Progressive version of civics is more traditional, drawing from its disenfranchised suffragist origins to note the imperative of an alert citizenry, empowered by quality information, to actively insist on accountable, representative government.[23]

The League of Women Voters also has a widely acknowledged legacy in regard to monitoring elections. In terms of democratic credentials, what could be more fundamentally cherished than encouraging everyone to vote? As volunteer advocates for the exercise of this national civic right, League members appear to be doing a public service of considerable value. But it turns out that the League's dedication to widespread voting may be its most contentiously political operation, due to starkly different interpretations of the electoral rights accorded by citizenship throughout American history and the extent to which the federal government dedicates itself to uphold their uniform protection. The League's predecessor NAWSA had been prepared before 1920 to find conditional voting constraints — such as race or education levels — as acceptable, if distasteful, qualifications for ballot rights *if* a majority of women made otherwise unachievable headway toward submitting official ballots as a result.[24] But the League of Women Voters has rejected that blot in NAWSA's history, coming down solidly for uniform, absolute voting rights for those enabled by law or under consideration for extension, advocating for the rigorous federal protection of rights for those vulnerable to disenfranchisement. This nonpartisan, if principled, position has placed the League in partisan waters, since voters needing protection (such as poor itinerants, immigrants, ethnic groups, blacks and youth) reliably vote Democratic.[25] The League regularly delivers argument to all government branches that energetic protection of electoral rights is a fundamental governmental role that should be handled on a nonpartisan, legally circumscribed basis.[26]

To kick these electoral positions into operational gear, the League of Women Voters asserts that more people will vote if associations independently supplement government-provided information on polling sites, ballot items, voter eligibility, and related voter services. While appearing bland and generic, elements of this League mission are often judged vital for citizens needing reassurance in order to gain practical poll access. They have become standard tools for both electoral organizers and prospective voters seeking respected independent information. True to its original purpose of getting women to the polls, the League of Women Voters still attempts to heighten and widen free and fair elections through assigning enthusiastic League members to registration tables, voter mobilization campaigns, advocacy visits on behalf of excluded voters, observation duties at district boundary settings, polling site monitoring stations, and local panels to explore new means to encourage free and fair elections.[27] These energetic, widespread efforts accord the League a priority slot for foreign dignitaries seeking to observe American democratic institutions deemed reputable, with the U.S. State Department's cooperation.

Voter judgment is repeatedly improved by the League of Women Voters through its longstanding series of nonpartisan candidate interviews and sponsored debates that clarify positions but withhold endorsement. The League's "Meet the Candidates," featured on national and local radio from 1928 to 1951 and followed by its televised presidential debates from 1952 to 1988, provided what came to be seen as a unique American public service through providing what participants considered a fair meeting ground within partisan divide.[28] But prospects for televised debates on these terms were compromised in 1988 by Democratic and Republican Party efforts to control terms of both engagement and subject matter, causing the League to withdraw debate sponsorship. Most recently, the League has provided the website VOTE411.org, which presents a comprehensive place-specific listing of election material. Its officers claim that fifteen percent of all voters accessed this website before voting in the 2008 election.[29]

While many Americans will predictably stay away on Voting Day, the League of Women Voters champions their *opportunity* to engage in the political process and further advocates for legitimate contests when they do.[30] Official voting levels may be beyond the League's responsibility, but its members attempt to increase voting numbers by addressing local issues judged of greatest communal importance, trying both to bridge residents' personal and political motivation to trek to the polls and to improve their judgment on arrival.

The League of Women Voters has had some historical success at reframing national electoral methodology. The excesses of the Nineteenth Century's Tammany Hall-style political manipulations were at least partially curbed prior to 1920 by Progressive campaigns to introduce the art of direct political persuasion and the encouragement of independent, non-affiliated voters.[31] Further development of these electoral shifts became one of the League's first programmatic priorities in the 1920s. It proceeded to champion the extension of American direct democracy, constraints on political party power, and wide distribution of rationally presented election information. But these nationally instituted Progressive reforms, while successfully advocated by the League, are insufficient to have improved contemporary voter judgment amidst new abuses by political parties and Super PACs. While the League's cumulative aim was to shift the tone of civic participation from partisan furor to respectful duty, American citizens appear to have returned, via loosened regulation of the public sphere, to Jacksonian emotionalism without the defense of strong party advocates.

The League of Women Voters also has a long history of voting rights campaigns to address the diversity of state electoral laws and the inconsistent, partisan character of their implementation and renewal.[32] This seemingly straightforward electoral work runs into passionate response on both sides of the spectrum. When the League charges local jurisdictions with inequitable participatory conditions and tries to empower disengaged and disadvantaged sectors, its reforming efforts may either be judged supportive of democratic principles or subversive to presently powered groups who benefit from incomplete turnout. There is a predictability in partisan positions regarding voting rights, with Republicans particularly prone to challenging liberalized rules as leading to fraud and Democrats charging voter ID cards and tightened registration procedures as constituting "the largest legislative effort to scale back voting rights in a century."[33] The League has until recently placed faith in the American judicial system to correct partisan misbehavior in the administration of democratic rights.[34] But the United States Supreme Court appears to have judged state discretion to trump national regulation, tacitly approving a narrowing of eligible voters toward the middle and upper classes by state fiat. As a recent example, the League presented arguments as Amicus Curiae for the League of United Latin American Citizens (LULAC) in their 2006 case before the Supreme Court, in the process challenging the obstructionist position of Texas Governor Rick Perry. Governor Perry won the case.[35] Such judgments indicate that the ongoing legal fight will be fierce and that the League may need a new strategy to succeed.

Opinion Formation

Curiously, the activity consuming most time within the League of Women Voters is the least known or appreciated outside its ranks. When people join their local Leagues, they are invited to plunge into ongoing policy groups that consider local ramifications of wide-ranging issues. The current agenda of the League's District of Columbia chapter, for example, features twenty-five such groups, studying subjects as various as crippled self-government, public land management, fiscal oversight, energy conservation, public education and mass transportation, to name a few.[36] In each case, member volunteers dedicate themselves to gathering reports and interviews from official and unofficial sources, supplemented by current demographic, economic, environmental and political facts that permit issue consideration from many points of view and afford discovery of previously unknown commonality across jurisdictions. In the process, the study groups radically expand subject-specific knowledge among active League members.

Where does all this knowledge go? Over time, the League of Women Voters has carved out a role Jean Schulte terms as "citizen expert" in which it "promot[es] civic activism and education while acting as a communication and information bridge between government officials and concerned citizens."[37] Its painstaking study-process eventually produces lengthy public reports that have provided the foundation for considerable bodies of legislation as well as informing whichever members of the public are paying attention. The League's currency to exhort the public for change, drawn from this earned stature, is applied to Congressional hearings, media coverage, and civic education programs in high school and elsewhere. In addition, the League adds to public awareness of brewing collective concerns. At the high point of its influence in the 1960s, the League's national alert on the dangers of water pollution, *The Big Water Fight,* was highly influential in making environmentalism a mainstream concern.[38] More recently, the League has co-hosted public examinations of The Red-Blue Divide, The Role of the Media in Politics, and The Changing Face of Power: Women in Politics.[39] The League increasingly contributes to allied efforts with other "good government" associations such as Common Cause to broaden public knowledge about subjects like Openness in Government: Looking for the Sunshine.[40]

Through these contributions to national conversation, the League of Women Voters attempts to fill the role of "public interest representative" by virtue of its process, non-vested position and knowledge. While the League is considered by other groups to be relatively "establishment" in process and method, it is distinctly reformist in study selection. Its members choose to use its respectability to air subjects that otherwise would not meet public scrutiny, aiming to represent missing citizen "stakeholders" at policy tables to present impacted views before officials rush to judgment. This function of League member duties is highly important at the local level, since stakeholder terminology relates to the distribution of finite and contested public resources like water, power, sewage and education. As a result, oppositional relationships between the League and other public and private parties can become dysfunctional in terms of both negotiated enlarged interest and eventual provision of public service.[41] Given that the League is not the only association dedicated to providing "public information," such public dialogue and assumption of public interest has been known to become highly contentious at all levels of government and community. Business and industry leaders are increasing adept at adopting similarly principled pose for radically different data sets, even taking time to charge the League with nondemocratic intent and faulty internal methodology.[42]

Does Progressive Advocacy Compromise Nonpartisanship or Public Interest Representation?

It is understandably confusing to the public that the nonpartisan League of Women Voters engages in energetic lobbying. How can such activity be nonpartisan if it has electoral effect? Does advocacy compromise the League's intent to operate in the public interest? Part of the answer lies in the character of its generalized lobbying principles, drawn from past Progressive Party platforms in support for open government, fair process and equitable representation. On one level, these reform quests are procedural. The League's argument is that government will be made more effective, representative and capable of resolving public problems responsibly if its existing structure becomes more fair and flexible to changing times through associated League advocacy. A senior Congressional staff member recently made passing conversation that, in his observation, the League is near unique among American lobbying groups through assigning its advocacy to causes of process. (The staffer concluded that this stance might protect the League from rancor targeted at other groups.) Yet the staffer is not entirely correct, for the League's history is also riddled with substantive campaigns, reflecting its adherence to redistributive versions of deliberative democracy in order to achieve equitable voice. Amy Gutmann and Dennis Thompson make these lines clear:

> Deliberative democracy . . . is about more than the *process* of deliberation alone. It is about substantive standards of *free and equal citizenship* and about the background conditions [of same] . . . if it is to function as well as it can . . . . When power is distributed unequally and when money substantially affects *who has access to the deliberative forum*, the results of deliberation in practice are likely to reflect these inequalities and therefore lead, in many cases, to unjust outcomes. [43]

As a result of this enlarged definition of fair process, the League of Women Voters has pushed for a bigger federal role in encouraging higher standards for American quality of life across the spectrum.[44] The League's nonpartisanship enters the mix through placing such advocacy outside direct association with political parties. It continues to avoid formal endorsement of any candidate.

Advocacy topics championed by any level of the League of Women Voters are not selected casually. They evolve from a long, inclusive, sometimes contentious, but in the end consensual process to select aspects of issues and particulars of solutions that are consistent with widely justifiable standards. Louise Young, historian of the League's extended operation, concludes in its defense, "the very process of consensus formation [yields] results that could be claimed as a fair approximation of public interest at any given juncture."[45] Selected targets tend to have been judged achievable in contemporary political climate, thereby crawling reform forward within specific jurisdictions; lobbying surges for grandly improbable national causes do occur, but with less frequency. Each local chapter will feature its own advocacy agenda, reached after considerable committee research and collective consideration. In the District of Columbia, the League's most energetic lobbying campaigns of the past decade have been on behalf of District voting rights and statehood, accountably rendered self-rule, local jurisdiction over gun control, and the equitable provision of improved public services.[46] These items represent a fair estimation of issues that *do* drive local politics in the capitol region, and the District's City Council members pay attention. The League's national-level advocacy positions, fashioned at its biennial conventions, will lack such specificity but show general collective cohesion.

Do Public Problems Get Solved in an Enlarged Fashion Through the League's Efforts?

It would be unrealistic to expect that most American associations could claim credit for effecting enlarged collective action, though many will make the claim. The primary reason is that even the most resolute, capable groups require an enabling political climate. Thus while the League of Women Voters' record is impressive, it is also inconsistent. In some eras, it could claim outright victory. Public health in teeming inner cities was advanced and disadvantaged voices were strengthened when the League achieved its first lobbying success with passage of the Sheppard-Towner Maternity and Infancy Protection Act in 1921. Civil service professionalism was promoted, patronage curtailed and middle-class bureaucrats enabled with passage of its championed Ramspeck Act of 1940. In other cases, more measured success came through shifting national opinion to enable a hope for future legislative advance. For example, in North Carolina during the 1970s, League members had successfully convinced many state residents that improving women's rights was a mainstream concern; yet ratification of the Equal Rights Amendment ultimately failed to pass the North Carolina

State Legislature. Through the League's ten-year fight for national ERA ratification, ground was laid to re-channel feminism — post defeat — into narrow goals which *did* progress toward educational, credit, sports and salary equity, each representing major redistributive shifts in social condition.[47]

There are most definitely eras in which the League of Women Voters' efforts are publicly and officially rejected. In spite of heady apparent advance of "good government" and "equitable representation" with the election of 2008, the League's current lobbying for protection of voting rights, nonpartisan redistricting, clean air standards, fair judiciary, and government accountability are, in terms of *its own* definition at least, going nowhere in the present United States Congress.[48] While this is directly attributable to the current deadlocked partisan balance within all branches of government, there will be major implications for the League's future efficacy as advocate for enhanced representative voice and democratic process.

Can one therefore draw a conclusion about narrowed impact that parallels the League of Women Voters' shrinking numbers? It depends upon the standards of consideration. The League is unquestionably good at what it does, presenting argument to the appropriate offices in the accepted fashion, with moral high ground on its side. In George Gallup's admiring past, the League could appear unstoppable when its members collectively agreed on an issue of *major* importance to them (see Chapter 6). This was particularly true when the League's efforts were strengthened by alliance with ad hoc public interest coalitions to hone in on specific targets.[49] For example, testimony rendered by League president Lee on 1950s civil liberties infringements helped make resistance to Senator Joseph McCarthy nonthreatening or even patriotic to the American public.

But contemporary operating conditions are becoming less friendly to such public interest success. The League of Women Voters had temporarily lost its nonprofit status under pre-1976 terms, restricting nonprofit lobbying to 10% of total operation, due to its advocacy on behalf of the ERA, but it was in good association company as groups on both sides of the issue struggled to stay within required constraints to receive tax-exemption.[50] The League had already concluded from that ERA fight that it could not successfully advocate goals American people were not yet ready to embrace, resolving in consolation to develop voters' opinions toward improved future wisdom.[51] So if one couldn't convince the American population with that 10% effort, the League attitude through 1980 was that perhaps success was not meant to be.

The national lobbying world has since been utterly transformed. Current lobbying regulations officially require all associations to be judicious to preserve nonprofit status, but the previous stringency was loosened to 20% with the Tax Reform Act of 1976 and further derailed by the 2010 Citizens United decision of the Supreme Court, which permits unlimited spending by both corporations and nonprofit groups on general topics. In the absence of accompanying requirements for disclosure of funding sources, shadow group operations with questionable grassroots foundation are swamping the airwaves with radical charges that distract the public and their Congressional representatives, reinforcing existing voice inequalities within the public sphere. The accustomed access of the League of Women Voters to public opinion formation is at direct risk from these changes.

Wobbles and Saves on the Democratic Bar

Up to this point, and in partial defiance of history, the League of Women Voters has generally rated quite well on a democratic scale defined in Chapter 3 and alluded to at the start of this chapter. It demonstrably enables its uniquely hyperactive members; provides internal and external training for democracy; extends the range of public critique to slipshod government administration; offers otherwise unavailable electoral service to voters; produces divergent interpretations to balance important decisions; strengthens disadvantaged voice through advocacy; deliberates and listens in good faith; and has almost uniquely democratic internal management.

Judgment on the League's operation gets slightly more complex in considering more closely the democratic culture parameters that contribute to the League's pursuit of public interest through individual efforts. In part because members set their standards so high, occasional evidence of their human capacity to hedge ideal choices, over-reach, disregard others' point of view, or be overly fierce in judgment of others might be of interest to the more plebian democratic rabble making no pretense for anything but self-interest.

One such vulnerability is in regard to understandable pursuit of organizational growth and resiliency. As the League of Women Voters represents *its version* of interest, it hopes to both politicize as many people as possible and encourage its own membership trends to reflect that range. To a degree, it tries to avoid attrition through selecting causes that won't disturb, alienate or result in member departure. Louise Young has observed, "Fostering political education implied reaching out for the greatest possible membership. If at the same time [League members] insisted on pursuing politically controversial legislation, the results would inevitably narrow the League's membership base."[52] But the League's additional insistence on advocacy inevitably affects those embracing its particular agenda. Time-specific selection can appear to serve the association's expansion yet embarrass its record through hypocrisy, for example via the League's exclusion of blacks during North Carolina's Civil Rights prelude.[53] In fairness, the considerable bulk of the League's historical record is one of impressively consistent principle, and it has settled for durably small membership while staying generally true to its Progressive (admittedly white-driven) origins. But if "public policy can only reflect the public interest to the extent that those who pressure the state are an accurate reflection of those who are affected by it," the League will be well served to increase diversification so as to demonstrably reach for deeper societal deliberation.[54]

The League of Women Voters has occasionally been capable of being its own worst enemy while presenting itself above "narrow regard" and championing the "less fortunate." From the organization's beginnings in 1920, members have purported to celebrate difference and reform the world. Often they live up to what could be judged their self-righteous trumpets. But recall for a moment the allure of an Americanized Mary Poppins entity arriving on the world stage. Convinced of its righteousness and excellent timing, a Poppinesque association — with accompanying naïve faith in the American version of democracy — can unintentionally exhibit condescension toward cultural, racial, class or activist difference on the basis of presumed expertise, rectitude and public applause. Megan Threkeld has presented historical material that makes some recalcitrant charges like Jane or Michael Banks justified if they reject the particular reforming call. Analyzing records of the first Pan American Conference for Women, hosted by the League of Women Voters in heady inaugural partnership with the U.S. State Department in 1922, she found ample evidence of active disregard and censoring of non-American attendees by League founder and American suffragist patron saint Carrie Chapman Catt, all in the name of her presumptive and under-informed vision, on that occasion at least, of American-led "international" female unity.[55]

An additional record of destructive personal interpretations of membership duties may cast light on shrinking expressions of appreciation for the League's current efforts, compared to its midlife heyday. Jean Schulte has suggested that the League actually contributed to its own marginalization as an association player within the 1970s' Environmental Movement through its members' condescending derision of emerging groups and the comparatively rigid methodology they brought to the collective table.[56] Such behavior, when it occurs, can undo not only bridging intent and impact but also an estimable public perception of the League's inner character.

In terms of inner dynamics within the League of Women Voters, there are also degrees of generational divides on appropriate forms of membership. Veterans of the suffragist and second-wave-feminist era in particular could be understandably self-congratulating for what were considerable campaigning accomplishments. A number of these members were observed to be dismissive toward younger, more cautious members. According to one League activist for the ERA, the veterans "used to terrorize you. They always thought you were such sissies because you wouldn't chain yourself to anything, wouldn't get arrested."[57] Such interaction could lead either to modeled behavior or resignation and foregone development, depending on the individuals.

While these critical snippets from the League of Women Voters' history are illuminating and important to unveil for full account, relative cultural mores and the likely existence of more egregious behavior from other concurrent associations suggest that human shortcomings should not be overestimated in this exploration of optimal civic association membership. The bulk of League materials record impressive, principled people volunteering their time to render their perception of best effort on behalf of the American people. The human aspect is only relevant to this rating to the extent it excludes, deprives, bleeds social trust or makes hypocritical the League's claim to be operating in the public interest. In respect to other associations' performance on these measures, the League will draw a positive, if not quite stellar, grade.

On the positive side of the democratic equation, the League of Women Voters is proud of its extended history upholding national adherence to domestic and international law.[58] Its established ability to pressure presidents, senators and bureaucrats through legitimate "front-door" channels has helped connect large gaps between authorized legislation and treaties and their administrative implementation. But it is unclear whether the League's record of consistent adherence to rules and watchful respect for rule-makers will continue to win the support of the general public. In a season turned on its democratic head, the vocal public appears to identify government collaboration with anti-citizen taint. This reputation, gained in part from playing by established rules, has sometimes affected the League's public influence as well as the viability of its alliance with oppositional, grassroots social movement groups for lobbying. Particularly as a result of frustrations experienced with government members on behalf of the Environmental Movement, some League members have concluded that cautious distance is appropriate due to mounting evidence of mishandled policy, botched administration and disregarded public interest by representatives at all levels of government.[59] Those "emerging" environmental protest groups actually taught the League a lesson, rather than the other way around.

The League of Women Voters' ninety-two year record of contributing to social capital appears to lodge in surprising places. While non-white members were not welcomed within the League's States-side halls until the late 1950s, its most Progressive pluralist stance has been toward the international community at large. While *individual* member style can intermittently mirror the naïve, jingoistic or even manipulative statements and actions on display within Threkeld's referenced 1922 Pan American Conference, *as an association*, the League can claim a large role in transforming American attitudes toward the oft-times challenging world throughout its long operation. Particularly crucial during the 1920s' Red Scare and the subsequent, long-lasting Cold War, the League's public education and advocacy efforts energetically sought for the United States to be a respectful, peaceful, law-abiding member of the international community (in keeping with its honoring of legitimized process), translating this stance into frontier support for the League of Nations, the World Court, the United Nations, disarmament and conflict resolution that stand, in Louise Young's terms, among its proudest achievements.[60] Such positions ultimately succeeded, at the height of its influence during the 1960s, in stretching American civics beyond the familiar local town to the remote African village, serving to encourage United States government institutions like the Peace Corps and changing world estimation of American character. Overlapping membership in the United Nations Association of the United States became predictable among League members. Contrary to Spider Web charges of the 1920s (see Chapter 6), radical international stances among members were unlikely.

Unfortunately, advocates of enhanced public participation are not always well served domestically by their cause. The League of Women Voters seems to be reliving a chapter from its Progressive forerunners. Its members have actively advocated easier voter registration, open government, citizen consultation, and voting rights enforcement to help vulnerable populations develop apace with those more favored. These measures are both used and countered within the United States by well-financed sectarian associations with public-sounding names, such as the Center for Representative Government, which argue, to increasingly successful effect, for tightened voting qualifications to theoretically avoid electoral fraud. In practice, such counter-measures intimidate those Americans less secure in Judith Shklar's sense of citizen entity, which refers to those with viable "social standing" and the requisite "agency and empowerment" to exercise rights as equals (see Chapter 2).[61] While the League envisions an energetically engaged citizenry as enabling the extension of democratic rights and equitable change, the narrowing participative field following its cumulative, backbreaking civic engagement campaigns ironically allows sectarian groups, and the citizens who support them, to begin undoing decades of Progressive legislation *with Progressive tools*. As James Madison could have forewarned League members, American public opinion has historically been fickle, unwise, or at worst dangerous. Some observers judge national public opinion to be "value neutral."[62] But deliberative democrats may be starting to wonder whether the United States political system is hopelessly value-biased in favor of fear-mongering elites who crowd out more mainstream concerns of the majority of the country.

Lessons in political realism are difficult for ardent idealists, even ones with healthy doses of pragmatism. But members of the League of Women Voters have been historically distinctive in drawing forward grounded assessments from their suffragist and second-feminist-wave campaigns to help assess the depth of their democratic challenge from forces of emotion, wealth and particularized interest. Their dogged interaction with both Republican and Democratic parties has helped the League advance its nonpartisan goals in the past. But Republican interest in participating in League efforts is flagging. Its party delegates consider themselves to be new forms of conservatives. "Process" as proposed by the League is seen by some of these party members as a vehicle for radical, minority-driven interest. Ironically, some of these conservative Republicans are presently upturning legislative process in order to retrench social welfare programs. Some League members are concluding that Progressive persuasion methods might be insufficient in the midst of unregulated power politics that empowers narrow, regressive groups terming themselves Eagle Forum, Moral Majority, Women Who Want to be Women or, most choice, Men Our Masters (naming a few anti-League groups from the ERA period).[63] League members are beginning to conclude that even "safe" procedural reform for the nation is becoming increasingly difficult to promote beyond the League's cocoon.

There will be partisan disagreement on whether the League of Women Voters has legitimately "attended to the common good" — one of Mark E. Warren's democratic associational ecology categories — in its advocacy, even given the consensual character of its process.[64] Theoretically, the League stands in good stead to meet deliberative democracy standards for reciprocal judgments that address the majority of parties impacted by concerns. But the precise identity and needs of the benefiting public emerging from policy processes for any distribution of public resources will always be contentious. The League's discipline toward constraint, specificity, deliberation and nonpartisanship helps reinforce its public focus and political role, but it does not always add excitement or eloquence to its reformist campaigns, nor does it ensure acceptance of its findings by the less disciplined public.

"Contributing to shared values"[65] — another of Warren's democratic ecology requirements — beyond the League's membership is a near-laughable expectation for associations in 2012's national season of "balkanized opinion" and established preference for identifying complaints over solutions.[66] But the League's persuasiveness may improve through drawing from its time-tested gender card, even in a changing society. Its traditional stance as a "social feminist" organization (it sought female advancement as part of an improving polity rather than full equity) has distanced League goals from those of feminist groups like the National Women's Party, which exclusively sought rights for women.[67] But female gender has always been inescapable, providing its name, most of its members, its reforming style, and its social welfare orientation. As Jean Schulte has found, maternalism can prove to be civically useful when so many other definitions and goals are contentious:

> Members [have] argued that their civic activities were not only necessary to create a better world for their children . . . but also to safeguard the promise of democracy in a nation founded on informed civic participation: To raise good citizens, a mother [has] had to be well-versed in the ideals and goals of active citizenship.[68]

This maternally enabling rationale for increased female engagement in democratic society as a means to preserve the nation's future is highly compelling to many people. It draws strength from apparently disabling results from "paternalism" gone awry and defies earlier female stereotypes of illogical emotionalism. Across the world, women are increasingly presented as arguably the best source for responsible civic reform. Yet it remains unclear whether the League's historically effective mantle of maternal "moral superiority" can continue to survive in a supposedly gender-neutral world.[69]

Does the League of Women Voters remain a dominant moral and political player in the civic world? Most associations will feature both vibrant and lackluster eras at various points in their histories, leading them to expand or retract their operation in reaction. At the risk of being unfair to the League's extraordinary record of accomplishment, it would be difficult to argue that it has been vibrant during the past decade. It is not invulnerable to changing national membership patterns amidst disappearing free time, reduced discretionary income and corroded democratic values. Impatient for results, some feminists have discounted the League's relevance for the past three decades, charging that its lengthy, consensual process wastes time, accommodates established power and becomes an end in itself. A similar charge could be leveled at other good government advocates. Some critics wonder whether the process focus of these groups is incapable of resolving the substantive playing field differences that durably resist equalization. As stakes are raised and time appears to drain away, extended internal conversations continue within the League on which is more important to members — the League as a means to reach a goal or an end in itself for the sheer experience of process. President Anna Lord Strauss had asserted during the League's 1940s reorganization, "the League is not an end in itself. It is a marvelous training ground."[70] Will its primary legacy be the training of democratic activists who form new versions of assembly in a post-League era? While Carrie Chapman Catt had hoped for expeditious politicization of women in the 1920s to awaken the country's civic engagement potential, the League's trademark project is clearly still incomplete.

Threatening times can provide a new lease on life for concerned people seeking purpose. The League's active advocacy of substantive issues does usually trump, by degree, concerns of retaining its membership and strengthens the loyalty of those who do remain. For these members, numerous democratic causes await in the process sphere itself, with voting rights under assault at both state and national levels by resurgent Republicans. The League is presently taking on the besieged electoral cause with a vengeance, allied with groups like Rock the Vote, whose leaders call voter ID and registration restrictions "a war on voting" as they prepare to launch defensive programs for impacted populations.[71] The League's reputation and sponsoring experience could be vital for that coalition's success.

Is the League of Women Voters Getting Rewarded For its Democratic Role?

Chapters 3 and 5 referenced measures of democratically laudable public interest groups and presented means by which they could be protected or rewarded to enhance positive impact. Some of these corrective actions include strengthening regulation of the nonprofit sector; enhancing public valuation for acts of citizenship; re-embracing legitimate democratic process; enforcing voting rights acts; shifting association operandi; and changing association structure to weather changed times. Peter Levine argues forcefully that the American government should not be neutral with respect to those associations playing important civic roles, and encourages vouchers that reward such volunteer activity as well as public funds for the associations' most beneficial functions.[72] (The only federal funds received by the League of Women Voters are from the U.S. State Department and the Library of Congress for international civil society forums and public diplomacy efforts.)[73]

There are additional nongovernmental forms such rewards or punishments could take. For example, historians could negatively judge the League of Women Voters' record in a manner which compromises future normative support for its operation. That is unlikely to happen. The League's record generally associates it with bipartisan achievements many people consider to be integral to the American democratic character. One of these achievements — contribution toward demonstrable advance in the status and capacity for the women it represents — actually hurts the League's ability to hold onto some of its members as they rise professionally and have less time to devote to voluntary efforts.

The League of Women Voters' traditional preference for avoiding the mainstream limelight may also contribute to a puzzling lack of public credit for ninety-two years volunteering on behalf of the country's supposedly most important concern.[74] While the League of Women Voters has historically received high public respect, increasingly disengaged citizens of both sexes may be too distracted or partisan to affirm its present incarnation.

Taking a general historical view, remaining members of the League of Women Voters might remind hovering doomsayers that cycles of decline and resurgence have been frequent since its founding in 1920, and that the League's major successes have occurred in seasons of national turmoil. Could it be that democratic decline could spell the League's rebirth? Perhaps, but conservative activists have empowered a shift toward particularized association and judicial siding with individual prerogative to the cost of collective capacity. This new "political opportunity structure" — in reference to the association sector's original choice of federated design to complement the sources of governmental decision-making — may be harder for the League to negotiate.[75] As the United States increasingly descends into verbal warfare reminiscent of pre-Civil War days, democracy's champion may need some help.

In an effort to discern whether the League of Women Voters was benefiting from its comparatively stellar performance on Mark E. Warren's aforementioned civic associational scale, Executive Director Nancy Tate was interviewed in May 2011 (refer to Appendix 3 for full author record of the interview).[76] When I referred her to statements by democratic theorists like Peter Levine that associations most beneficial to democracy should receive some kind of favorable treatment, she responded that there is no evidence of a trend in that direction. (In fact, the League is more subject to *penalty* by the Internal Revenue Service because of lobbying limits for nonprofit organizations.) During the last several years, the League has been increasingly vulnerable to abuse from bonded, partisan organizations. For example, during 2009 the League of *American* Voters (italics added) was formed to combat the emerging Patient Protection and Affordable Care Act, then under national consideration, using almost identical masthead and twisting familiarly phrased principles of the League of Women Voters with radically different intent. The League of Women Voters challenged the new group for misrepresentation, even sending members to its physical door and finding it to be a shadow operation. Filing a complaint, the League of Women Voters was then deluged with hate mail and forced to hire guards for its national office. Government officials have not acted in its defense. Reward for the League's service may be consigned to historians, though political theorists could find possible martyrdom of an organization unusually effective at producing democratic values and practices a bad sign indeed.

Part III

The Stakes

8

Conclusion:

The Argument for Sustaining Particular Democratic Associations

Those Americans who can still afford subscriptions have not stopped joining associations. But their prevailing choices have not been faithful to an American myth that self-rule is plural, diverse or morally responsible. To realize that fantasized vision, joiners would select associations that provide communal experience within diversity, enable enlarged judgments on the part of the public or contribute to clear and justifiable instruction from identifiable publics to government institutions. In reality, American citizens fuel a wide array of what Robert D. Putnam has termed tertiary associations, funded by passive but generous donors, with lobbying messages that derive from professionalized hierarchy rather than member-driven experiential process.[1] The lack of counterbalance to this trend encourages a contest of specific interests without the benefit of public accountability, overpowers the less organized or financed participatory groups and fails to give expression to individual member voices. While purporting to solve public ills, these tertiary associations, ranging from conservative-oriented Americans for Prosperity to liberal-inclined Move On, may indeed augment united, purposeful voice in the political process. But they can also cement inequality, promote selective obstruction of civic rights, simplify public argument for the sake of private gain, and fail to provide "members" with an authentic deliberative experience. The crux of these present association trends is that they pair dismal public participation with both irresponsible governance and misaligned policy, thus impacting the heart of democracy.

There are different models of associated participation. Chapters 2 and 3 reviewed Progressive-derived public interest associations, which have been designed to address persistent societal imbalance by representing wider population swaths and timeframes in the theory that voter judgment, representative decisions, and public performance will improve as a result. Civic groups like the League of Women Voters are particularly rare in the scale of their ambitions and performance, even by these exacting public interest group standards. As shown within Chapters 6 and 7, few associations have shown the durability, success or democratic import of the League over the course of its ninety-two year history. Dedicated to activating all voters and improving their judgment, directly schooling active members and the general electorate on democratic procedure, and relying on grassroots deliberation toward collective solutions, the League's members embody a process-oriented pursuit of Alexis de Tocqueville's "self-interest properly understood." If one were to read a tourist brochure about America, surely a direct descendant of righteous suffragists — proven to operate democratically, develop its members' civic capacity, and reform democratic institutions — would be held as a national treasure, protected and preserved for the benefit of future generations.

Debatable Legacy

While the League of Women Voters is unquestionably singled out for periodic public applause because of these tangible democratic merits, its associated enterprise is struggling to survive while numerous sectarian, hierarchical and democracy-disabling groups are thriving. This is in part because the precepts it accepts as given do not represent uniformly cherished national values.

While our democracy exporters may blur the stubborn challenges we share as a nation with developing democracies, the fact remains that the very concept of citizen participation is highly contentious in the United States. The current American system is largely designed to handle delegated civic authority with only occasional public participation, presuming actualization of the people's will through election day tallies and government process. Progressive era reforms may have launched some direct democracy elements, but elitist power politics continue to define most electoral and legislative success. Political operators can be brutal in corralling only those members of the public who will advance their cause. Even informed reformers may judge citizen disengagement as less than disastrous if ignorant unpredictability is avoided in the voting booth. Other players may welcome low turnout if the resulting representation more reliably advances their interests by virtue of those who forgot, chose not to show, or were blocked along the way.

The expanding divide between what Americans are reputed to celebrate in democratic theory and what they choose to cultivate in daily life is essentially a rejection of the presence of "one nation" alluded to in every pledge of allegiance. Public opinion swings on whether public-interest membership associations like the League of Women Voters are laudable, let alone sustainable, because of disagreement, particularly fierce in an era of financial straits, about the precise identity of those civic members designed to receive scarce or commonly-held public resources.

There is also far-ranging public disagreement with the League of Women Voters and other groups on the position that Americans remain an improvable population. Recent evidence is unpromising. Given widespread opportunity to participate in public forums on health reform prior to Congressional passage of the Patient Protection and Affordable Care Act in March 2010, citizens across the country repaid the favor with violent shouting matches and durably ignorant expressions of hate and distrust. Human development above such lows requires opportunity, which translates to time, self-sufficiency and education that is beyond practical reach for large portions of the population. Many people who believe they celebrate American civic life will not support such opportunity for other people, preferring vague displays of the national flag and guarding against incursions on their own resources.

Throughout its history, the League of Women Voters has rejected such civic boundaries, resisted negative branding of opposition and held to its cautious faith in Americans' developmental capacity, a testimony to the virtues of a long, careening history through liberalized and reactionary national eras. Like John Stuart Mill in the Nineteenth century, the League's members aim to bridge private with public lives, believing that the former compel the latter, which in turn transform original self-interested motivations toward enlightened senses of greater cause.[2] Their uneven success has made them aware that historically, "the rights for citizen participation . . . have turned out to be value-neutral"[3] and capable of advancing regressive minority cause. American pursuit of individual rights and the accountability and regulation that protect their exercise will predictably conflict. Still, League members return year after year because of a faith that fine-tuning democratic process will make civic engagement as equitable, developmental, and inclusive as possible.

Some of these divided societal attitudes do appear to contribute toward slow League of Women Voters decline in a consumer-driven joining market. It is no longer fashionable to be a member. To be cited on League rosters, members are almost always active on the local level, which is increasingly difficult for a busy and transient population. But civic-minded people, while always small in numbers, doggedly continue to seek bridging centers for public activism. As Chapter 6 made clear, the League's membership has stayed remarkably stable *on a national level* relative to other membership associations. This is primarily due to the expressive activation of League members' values, consistently linking to some version of altruistic class-bridging purpose. The effect of these personal values as channeled through League volunteer functions extends far beyond the narrowly circumscribed joining populations, which gives deep satisfaction to the impressively loyal membership. While most members age beyond 60, highly engaged younger members also exist. They also indicate a determination to carry the participatory suffrage legacy forward in traditional hands-on manner (see Chapter 6 for recent profiles). The durable attraction of this normative motivation for Sidney Verba's distinctive few (see Chapter 4) encourages a viable future for the League in spite of shifting civic culture.

But the League is not invincible, particularly at its trademark grassroots level. As an indicator of shifting trends, the League of Women Voters of Oregon had historically been a strong chapter, reflecting the strength of the western Suffragists, their 1912 success in the state, and the subsequent civic proclivities of the urbanized western coastal strand population. LWV of Oregon's state-level survival is now in considerable doubt as its numbers plummet at an unusually high League rate. *Six (out of twenty-three) of its local Leagues have disbanded since 1981. Two thirds of the remaining Oregon Leagues have less than fifty members.* Statewide, LWV of Oregon membership is down by 30% within thirty years, a much faster decline that the incremental national League pattern.[4]

While the League of Women Voters is celebrated as an extended grassroots institution, it is hard not to argue that the national span of its localism is fighting a losing battle. Some local chapters like Centre County, Pennsylvania continue to thrive (see Chapter 6), helping drive the national League figures which remain stubbornly resilient in comparison to other civic groups facing empty chambers. But many state chapters of the League face the prospect of significant consolidation, causing aging members to travel considerable distance for attendance while addressing agendas that are less local and personally relevant. This may make it harder to bridge the private and the public through the League's original model (see Chapter 6). Adding such travel to already tightened time and money constraints, those members who find farther travel difficult may resign at faster rate.

Paths Toward League Resurgence

Since 1920, the League of Women Voters has traveled through numerous cycles that skirted its organizational disaster through partisan divide, financial distress, reactionary targeting and a disinterested population amidst laissez faire regulation. The operating climate for associations has fundamentally changed since the Jacksonian and Progressive eras that gave many of them birth. Pluralistic divisions, changing female aspirations, and evaporated volunteer time are but a few recent societal alterations that impede the League's physical assembly for common action. But there are a number of ways the League could revive both its membership and its purpose for a healthier future.

The first step is practical and achievable. General association engagement in the American public arena could be made more fair through strengthened, rational government regulation of the nonprofit sector — standardizing rules, instituting financial curbs, providing guidelines for what constitutes extreme messaging, and actively monitoring full disclosure, fair practice and democratically-consistent operation within any association receiving 501c3 or 501c4 benefits. A highly meaningful innovation would be the narrowing of official definition for "association" to those groups with active volunteer members and separate tax category to match (see Chapter 5 for description of this area).

The second method is in theory fundamental yet in practice quite challenging. Ailing civic culture is causing the concept of representative, national-scale democracy to lose individualized meaning. Public-spirited action is very difficult as a result and likely to be drowned out by James Madison's worst nightmare of narrowly informed factions unleashed. But revival of widespread civic education could shift the public focus back toward common purpose. Helpful reforms in this regard would include heightened valuation of bridging civic acts and attitudes. Discipline should be considered for behavior that disables democratic process when entities are accorded official civic role. A fundamental widening of public participation could be achieved through establishing voting holidays for all jurisdictions. Public discourse and fairness could be improved by establishing clear ground rules for civic engagement vehicles like town halls. Finally, Americans can be further encouraged through media and education efforts to face up to the reality of multi-ethnic, split-class citizenship as a collective identity and to acknowledge the difficulties faced by some Americans when attempting to exercise their civic rights. Such a reinvigorated civic culture would also reward those associations whose membership actively promotes individualized experience of democracy on a daily private and public basis. Compensation could conceivably be directed toward qualifying associations themselves, for example through communication subsidies to equalize voice on public channels. Alternatively, vouchers might be sent directly to members for public service activities such as polling monitors and high school registration. Conceivable payment or penalty of any form aside, the League of Women Voters' most important return for any positive shift would be an enabling culture that might finally acknowledge fuller appreciation for the League's services and behavior, largely unrewarded and frequently obstructed for close to a hundred years.

The third revival approach is to try yet again at what has become a misnomer, effecting "good government" through a particular focus on democratic process. In addition to fair procedure, "good government" can refer to a range of reforms that address accountability, public management quality, democratic structure mutability, popular sovereignty character, and effective political equality. The Progressive Era that helped spawn the League of Women Voters also launched deliberative democracy as a process-oriented "good government" theory that systematically seeks a common good. Some theorists dismiss this field as "democracy for the sake of democracy."[5] Yet without it, there is little room for moving beyond polarized politics and eventual popular discontent on a massive scale. Deliberative democrats reject politics as power play, insisting America's normative dedication to "liberty, freedom and justice for all" on a mutually reciprocal basis can only be realized through uniform embrace of fair procedures.[6] Clearly, the League is not alone in asserting that the public interest must be experienced through reciprocal engagement. Robert Dahl has argued that "the common good resides in the practices, institutions, and processes that . . . promote the well-being of ourselves and others . . . . "[7] As noted by Mark E. Warren, public interest groups like the League therefore have a vital role to play in effecting a national deliberative process that connects the public to both the formation of policy and the administration of services.

> The deliberative elements of a democracy can only be organized along associational lines and the deliberative publics can only emerge where there exists social bases in voluntary associations.[8]

As one of the few viable national membership groups still focusing on civics, the League earnestly advances a rational participatory vision of America in the faith such change will eventually emerge if public passivity toward failing democratic institutions is overcome.

The fourth path to League of Women Voters renaissance is through astute tapping of citizen discontent to gain new, highly concerned members prepared for activism on behalf of democratic process. John Mark Hansen observes that League membership has historically risen at times of deep public concern.[9] The League's unrelenting fight for women's ability to exercise civic rights is a powerful legacy that has extended to helping other vulnerable populations. This stance has significant consequences, since knowledge of civic rights and the state of the union leads to power, then to political inclusion, empowering membership and the voting public to improve both democratic responsiveness and societal equity.[10] Increasingly, the League is joining with other civic associations to advocate for universal protection of active citizenship. If nativist state-level trends continue to be championed by various governors and legislators, the League's righteous counter-effort will become highly partisan and may test its nonpartisan brand.

As discussed in Chapter 7, the League of Women Voters is already gaining new steam from countering a resurgent "war on voting" that seeks to restrict voter registration, tighten qualifying ID requirements and puncture individual recourse for procedural abuse. Nothing could be more threatening to this association's fundamental purpose of enabling civic participation. Carrie Chapman Catt had delivered a revolutionary message on the occasion of the Nineteenth Amendment's passage in 1920:

> The vote is a power, a weapon of offense and defense... Use it intelligently, conscientiously, prayerfully... [to] serve the common good.[11]

In a sense, obstructionist activists have provided the League with a recruitment gift as they seek to manipulate their way to electoral victory. Newly inspired, League members are energetically devising new strategies to encourage diverse turnout and provide defense to those challenged at the booth. This aspect may indeed expand the League's generational attraction, since younger voters are among the impacted populations.

Shifting operational conditions may suggest a benefit in shifting the League's "congenial" organizational style. Clamor may be needed for fair contestation. As Amy Gutmann has observed,

The politics of mutual respect is not always pretty... Citizens may find it necessary to make extreme and uncompromising statements... These strategies may be justified when for example, they are necessary to gain attention for a legitimate position that would otherwise be ignored...[12]

Suffragists learned in the fight for the Nineteenth Amendment that passion merited a place in both public discussion and problem resolution, both in recognition that it was frequently inevitable on all sides in the former and in perception that it proved effective on behalf of the less powerful in the latter.[13] Exhibition of this emotion is not new to otherwise rational-appearing League members, perhaps because of a mix of moral conviction and shared assertiveness. Personal reservoirs of passionate advocacy empower sustained membership and have led some local Leagues to shift tactics toward provocative actions that garner public attention to the cause.

Since 1924, the League of Women Voters has held that "the [agenda] Program is the thing."[14] Guttman would agree that the principle political battleground arises from setting the public agenda. To make such agenda-setting fair and informed, she argues for principles of preclusion, reciprocity and basic opportunity.[15] The League can use this theoretical argument to enhance the public's appreciation for its deliberative identification of important public topics. Procedural agenda activity can drive judicious advocacy for otherwise neglected issues, help private citizens insist on shifting stalled public institutions away from peripheral special-interest minutiae and, like in 1924, give League members reason to stay involved (see Chapter 6). This method of League resurgence essentially recharges its essence, and blends well with people seeking to "restore" America to storied progressive responsibility.

The League of Women Voters can also gain members by capitalizing on a growing grassroots movement across the political spectrum to reclaim popular sovereignty over government process. Both Republican and Democratic members, and some party officials, argue for procedural reform to protect a fair democratic playing field. The League's internal operation and external advocacy display insistence that democratic process is a tool —not a Bible — that should be deliberated and amended to fit circumstance and social need. Without access to procedural change through agreed means, minority parties can lack confidence that their position is factored into the eventual "sense of the group" so successfully rendered within the League's proceedings.[16] While distanced contemporary viewers can understandably disparage American capacity to honor process in a principled and equitable fashion, mutability was a founding Constitutional principle deemed essential for its ratification in 1789. Active League membership provides vigorous training in process utilization to achieve shifting democratic goals. Those critics legitimately seeking procedural reform could expressively demonstrate those values through plunging into League efforts to put principles into action.

An additional reconstructive path toward continued survival of the League of Women Voters might improve organizational sustainability through tinkering with the League's federated membership structure. Peter Levine and John D. McCarthy consider chapter structures to have been historically important for extending, through franchise association, association identity and democratic impact (see Chapter 5). Indeed, federation webs have dramatically helped extend the League's impact in the past (see Chapter 6). As Mark E. Warren has noted, grassroots-oriented federated structure indicates a democratically relevant organizational commitment to individual member development as a path toward achieving association goals (see Chapters 3 and 4). But in practice, some League members — dedicated not only to democratic process but also to advocacy and sustainability — now privately find the League's structure overwhelming and overly slow in a fast-paced contemporary environment. If the fate of the League of Women Voters of Oregon is any indication (see the beginning of this chapter), the League of Women Voters of the United States' best prospect for national survival might ironically be as a centralized protest business with fewer, less engaged volunteers members (see Chapter 5). It is, however, difficult to picture League members becoming a "nonlucrative distraction."[17] On the positive side, such reorganization would conceivably spur professionalized retention of purpose to fight on contributors' behalf. David Vogel argues, "The only way that one can really live as a 'public citizen' is to make a living at it... making opposing business into a business."[18] On the negative side, such centralized direction and professionalized operation would make it harder for individual members to be heard and develop through community. Given the established relation between an association's structure and purpose and its members' motivation to join and stay, altering the structure would likely result in significant member flight. While the League of Women Voters might become more efficient, audible or competitive in a professionalized pursuit of organizational purposive goals, its near unique democratic contribution rendered through volunteerism and legitimate representation would, in member loss, noticeably diminish.

Weighing Disbandment

It is presently unclear whether government and civil society should routinely be neutral while associations with proven civic benefits struggle to remain in existence. Nancy Rosenblum essentially argues for Darwinian life cycles.[19] But given the stakes for fair democratic participation and governmental accountability, passivity may not be neutral if the League of Women Voters' decline is unabated. While "the moral uses of pluralism" may encourage individual choice — and indeed, the League is not for everyone — Rosenblum's caution that selective favor would "legislate schools of virtue" seems odd if the League's virtues in question are inscribed throughout the American colonies' Declaration of Independence and the United States Constitution.

Theoretical arguments for life support on the basis of the League of Women Voters' superior democratic character may be irrelevant if financial support or viable membership literally die out. In that case, other American engagement vehicles will probably remain. There are plenty of advocacy groups representing prospective voters, disadvantaged or otherwise. In fact they seem to be everywhere. Many groups attempt to educate the public about pressing collective concerns, though it can be difficult to assess the quality of their information or the character of their operation. Concern with democratic process is not unique to the League; Common Cause could carry the torch. Nonpartisan voting protection could be undertaken by the Brennan Center for Justice and Rock the Vote.

But where the League of Women Voters is unique and irreplaceable is in the combination of advocacy, education and civic rights through developmental process within its own membership-intensive ranks as well as process guardianship for national democratic institutions. Recall the League heyday of the 1940s and 1950s referred to in Chapter 6: when a small collection of civic-minded women in North Carolina towns sought a vehicle that could enlarge and strengthen their communities through democracy, they personally plunged in to form their own little chapter of the League of Women Voters at tremendous effort, for it presented the obvious and only choice.[20] The League may remain alone in that role today.

Mountain Versus Molehill

To some extent, it is a stretch to attach significant concern to whether the League of Women Voters survives or folds. Its membership is miniscule compared to large groups like the American Civil Liberties Union. Speaking realistically, one association — no matter how civic — cannot improve the country's engagement dynamic; only a shift in national culture that celebrates diversity, deliberation and active citizenship can do that. Besides, civic participation was never intended to be pervasive in the United States; at best, citizens have been positioned to serve as sensors.[21] Perhaps the League's expectations of potential citizen behavior are unreasonable and unnecessary. Human judgment is frequently erratic, even when guided by process. If public opinion is, as Alexis de Tocqueville feared, beyond redemption as strange and without rational explanation — let alone positive content — civic education may be hopeless. People turn out to vote in regrettably small numbers, but they've done so regardless of whether they are supposedly contributing to competitive elitist democracy, power politics, plutocracy, or whatever the fashionable disaster theory may be, so intervening in the dynamic could be considered useless.

In a similar vein, League of Women Voters closure would not end association linkage of civil society and government. The remaining association players may be lacking in clear volunteer character or local support, but they certainly deliver an expression of somebody's interest. Yet it is precisely the self-interested, procedure disregarding, memberless direction, and public resource mismanagement of that thriving "self-rule" that is at issue. If indeed these thriving political-oriented shadow associations are the incubators of America's democratic norms and serve as dominant sensors for public policy, a conceivable demise of the League of Women Voters might suggest a new season of self-first, entirety-never.

One could also argue there are other ways to civically partici- pate besides joining associations, such as responding to polls, at- tending town halls, performing community service, and independ- ently following the development of relevant issues. The problem here is that people who join civic groups have also been demon- strated to engage in those alternative acts. Civic behavior multiplies itself, and its absence on the association roster is likely to duplicate in the other civic forms.

America's association landscape has profoundly changed in the last forty years. Recent conservative administrations have fash- ioned for nonprofit advocacy groups what Paul Pierson and Theda Skocpol term a "new political opportunity structure" with "new technologies and models of association building" that benefit a "redistribution of political voice" particularly toward conservative populists, ironically increasing government size while asserting ideals of American unity gone-by at the expense of social welfare.[22] Judith Shklar's vision of American citizenship as uniformly afford- ing "a demand for inclusion in the polity" is being significantly nar- rowed.[23]

Pierson and Skocpol argue that reduced viability of bridging membership-driven associations has "diminished democracy" through realigning collective assets toward privatized identities, values and aims. The paucity of stable public-oriented membership groups leads, in their view, toward "the attenuation of shared citi- zenship and equal opportunity in America's future."[24] As grassroot trends decline, "public interest" will in this view inevitably take on a more elitist tinge driven by the informed, educated professionals who dedicate themselves to its advancement. The public interest appears to have left the mainstream of American sentiment so suc- cessfully channeled by the League of Women Voters in the past.

What the League of Women Voters seeks most fundamentally — and what is at primary risk should it fail — is a closer relation- ship between the original sovereignty vested in the popular government and the recognized justice of its actions. The most important democratic aspect of public participation is informed assent. Jürgen Habermas explored the meaning of different levels of private assent to public actions. It can derive from outright coercion, tradition, apathy, pragmatic acquiescence, instrumental acceptance, normative agreement or, finally, ideal normative agreement. Assent does not bode well for vibrant democracy — be it domestic or across the seas from America — until it reaches some normative form.[25] When Americans ratified the Constitution in 1789, they did so instrumentally, in order to achieve the realization of particular interests through common unity. The lack of deeply held common values in that relatively homogenous society became even less binding over the subsequent centuries as pluralism took off through immigration, growing inequality and societal complexity, causing a majority of the country to now feel apathetic, constrained or pragmatically willing to be manipulated. Yet only normative agreement can breed the sort of active consent Tocqueville believed he glimpsed within the American population. To achieve that positive goal within this divided climate, "the source of legitimacy is not the pre-determined will of individuals, but rather the [open-ended and continuously learning] process of its formation, that is, 'deliberation itself.'"[26] That form of legitimacy amounts to a definition of the League of Women Voters' history and promise, underlining a judgment that it should be protected from some form of Camelot-like fate through closer appreciation of its contributions to democracy.

Appendix 1

Change in Membership of the League of Women Voters, the General Federation of Women's Clubs and the National Society of the Daughters of the American Revolution as a Percentage of the Total U.S. Population

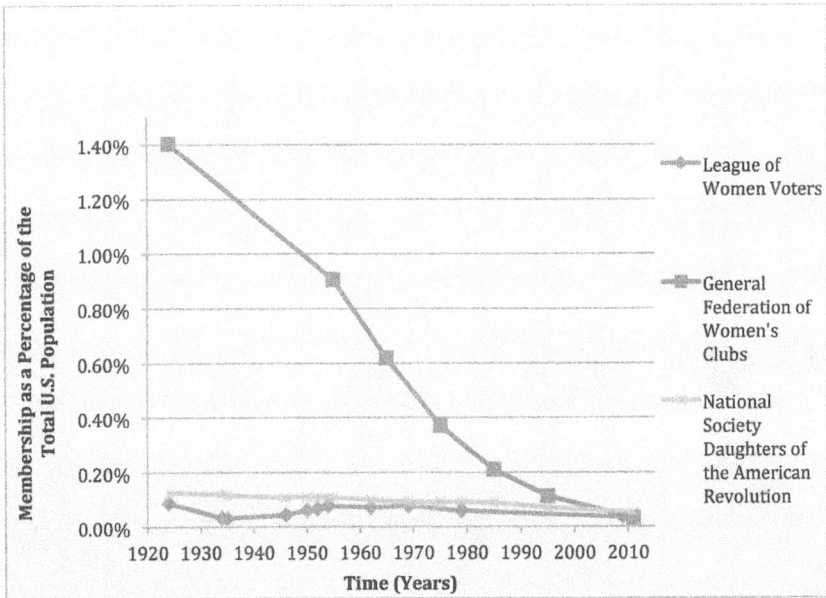

Appendix 2

Change in Membership of the League of Women Voters as a Percentage of the Total U.S. Population

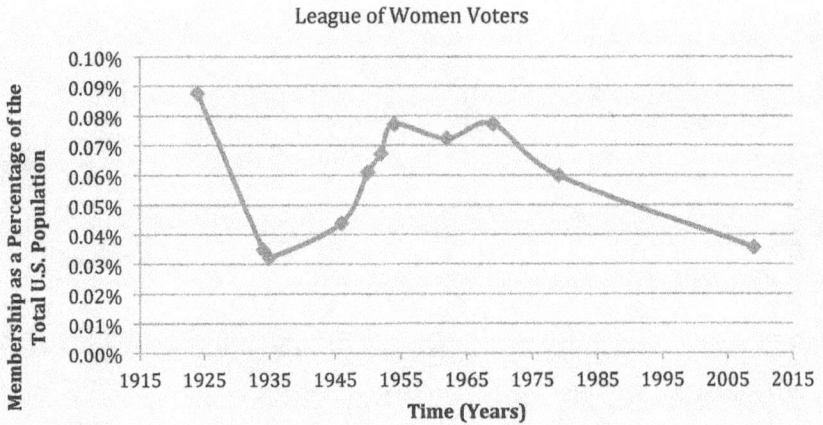

Appendix 3

Author's Record of Interview with Nancy Tate, Executive Director of the League of Women Voters

Looking at sustainability in terms of member numbers and finances, do either affect the League's program effectiveness and how?

Nancy Tate commented that League administrators are not sticklers at the national level in terms of defining members to be only those who formally join and get active within the local Leagues. (The local Leagues, though, do stick to those definitions, so their numbers will be different.) If both members and supporters are counted, the current number is 140,000. It used to be that one could join at either the local or national level. That was changed within the last two years to local-joining only.

There is a Membership Recruitment Initiative (MRI) that has been operative for the last several years wherein the national office, with the help of professional consultants, provides expertise to local chapters to expand their membership, training them to grow. Thirty-two state Leagues are helped this way.

Fundraising is challenging. Twenty-four percent of their funding comes from dues. The only federal money comes through (1) the State Department for the Global Democracy program and (2) the Library of Congress for the World Leadership program, which recently engaged with Tunisia and Cuba. Most foundations do not fund general American democracy initiatives, preferring to favor those that target specific populations. The League does get support from the Carnegie Corporation for Vote 411 and from American Express for work in five cities where the corporation has call centers and wants to be seen as responsive. Anonymous donors support election reform through the League at the state level. Community foundations almost always support at the local level only. So the national division of the League is very dependent on special contributions.

What are the prospects for confederated structure in a protest business age?

Tate was surprised to hear confederated structure is back in theoretical vogue (see Chapter 5). Confederated structure is awkward bureaucratically; though League members and staff accept it as defining who they are, they don't totally celebrate it. She sounded a little envious of Common Cause, which doesn't have to be as attentive to its members and may be more effective as a result. It would be hard for other groups to activate members in the same way; it takes long evolution, sustained attention, and a certain character for the agenda.

Is the character of member engagement changing? How are younger members being drawn in?

See MRI. People need to learn to share and bring themselves and their chapters up to date. If they ask for help, the national office is prepared to step in, for example by getting people comfortable to intentionally ask people to join the League. They need feedback, and a support system. The Ruth Shur Training Program helps empower members to develop in this direction.

It appears that the education, activation and advocacy functions of the League have remained consistent over its [then] 91 years. True? Has technology transformed the delivery?

Advocacy has always been an important element of the League's operation. It has to be drawn from forty-two national policy areas that have received official approval through painstaking consensual process engaging members at all levels. Tate frequently encounters public misunderstandings regarding League advocacy, including those who believe the League can't take lobbying positions and remain non-partisan. She points out that the League never limited itself to services like voter registration, and has always, in addition, taken stands on issues. But it never endorses candidates.

But for the local Leagues to take stands, they have to arrive at them by democratic process. For example in regard to immigration, the national League office couldn't say anything until local Leagues contributed to national resolution of a League position. This is time-consuming democracy in action.

Technology will become more and more important. There will be fewer and fewer mailings. Given who they serve, what they are trying to achieve, and the extent of their funding, they consider themselves without choice but to go heavy on technology and virtual presence. There will be a new website this summer, featuring blogging, which seems to work very well.

Democratic theorists argue that associations most beneficial to democracy should receive some kind of favorable treatment. Do you see that happening?

No. The League is very vulnerable to abuse from other organizations and government officials don't step up in its defense. For example, in 2009, the League of *American* Voters was formed to combat the health reform bill under almost identical masthead. The League of *Women* Voters challenged them, even going to their physical door and finding it a shadow operation. Filing a complaint, the League was deluged with hate mail and hired guards for the national office.

What are your most valuable alliances? Have they helped achieve some otherwise elusive successes?

Everything is done in partnership, though few partnerships extend across the board; they tend to be specific. Most give next to no return and draw most from the League's reputation to assist others. For example, the YWCA and the Junior League are both "paper partners," sharing facilities with the League across the country. For an issue like election finance reform, the League teams up with Common Cause and others.

Notes

Chapter 1

1. Alexis de Tocqueville, *Democracy in America,* J.P. Mayer, ed., George Lawrence, trans. (New York: Harper Perennial, 1969), 506-508, 525.
2. Mark E. Warren, *Democracy and Association* (Princeton: Princeton University Press, 2001), 4. Italics added.
3. Ibid., 3.
4. Robert D. Putnam, *Bowling Alone: The Collapse and Revival of American Community* (New York: Simon and Schuster, 2000), 156.
5. Warren, *Democracy and Association,* 149.

Chapter 2

1. Ibid., 3.
2. Ibid., 206.
3. Grant Jordan and William A. Maloney, *Democracy and Interest Groups* (New York: Palgrave Macmillan, 2007), 193.
4. Ibid., 7. Italics added.
5. Mark E. Warren, "The Political Role of Non-profits in a Democracy," *Society* 40, no. 4 (May/June 2003): 48, 51.
6. Judith Shklar, *American Citizenship: The Quest for Inclusion* (Cambridge: Harvard University Press, 1991), 3. Italics added.
7. Samuel L. Popkin and Michael A. Dimock, "Political Knowledge and Citizen Competence," in *Citizen Competence and Democratic Institutions,* ed. Steven L. Elkin and Karol Edward Soltan (University Park: Pennsylvania State University Press, 1999), 117; and Roger Wachbroit, "The Changing Role of Expertise in Public Deliberation," in *Civil Society, Democracy and Civic Renewal,* ed. Robert K. Fullenwider (Lanham: Rowman and Littlefield Publishers, 1999), 356-57. Popkin and Dimock judged it is acceptable for people to be imperfectly versed because they use associations for "information shortcuts" and "political cues" with basic contextual knowledge. Wachbroit cautioned that voluntary

associations might seek to "enlarge" and "educate" the public's limited expertise but may not have deserved their trust, since "expert" facts were fallible and frequently partisan-driven.

8. Marion Smiley, "Democratic Citizenship: A Question of Competence?" in *Citizen Competence and Democratic Institutions*, ed. Steven L. Elkin and Karol Edward Soltan (University Park: Pennsylvania State University Press, 1999), 372-377.

9. Alison Kadlec and Will Friedman, "Deliberative Democracy and the Problem of Power," *Journal of Public Administration* 3, no. 1, art. 8 (2007): 16; and Warren, *Democracy and Association*, 79.

10. Nancy Rosenblum, "Navigating Pluralism: The Democracy of Everyday Life (and Where it is Learned)," in *Citizen Competence and Democratic Institutions*, ed. Steven L. Elkin and Karol Edward Soltan (University Park: Pennsylvania State University Press, 1999), 68.

11. Amy Gutmann and Dennis Thompson, *Why Deliberative Democracy?* (Princeton: Princeton University Press, 2004); David Held, *Models of Democracy* (Stanford: Stanford University Press, 2006), 232; and Norman Frolich and Joe A. Oppenheimer, "Values, Policies, and Citizen Competence," in *Civic Competence and Democratic Institutions*, ed. Steven L. Elkin and Karol Edward Soltan (University Park: Pennsylvania State University Press, 1999), 162-183.

12. Virginia A. Hodgkinson and Michael W. Foley, ed., *The Civil Society Reader* (Hanover: University Press of New England, 2003), xxiii; and Mansbridge, "On the Idea That Participation Makes Better Citizens," 305. Hodgkinson and Foley record Putnam's conclusion that engagement widened knowledge and compassion that reduce the costs of collective governance and trust. Mansbridge quoted Tocqueville's reference to an opinion he shared with J.S. Mill.

13. Benjamin Barber, *A Place for Us: How to Make Society Civil and Democracy Strong* (New York: Hill and Wang, 1998), 42-43.

14. Jordan and Maloney, *Democracy and Interest Groups*, 17. In reference to Robert Dahl.

15. Warren, *Democracy and Association*, 149.

16. David Knoke, "Associations and Interest Groups," *Annual Review of Sociology* 12 (1986): 1. Knoke used the term several years before Mark E. Warren.

17. Theda Skocpol, "The Tocqueville Problem: Civic Engagement in American Democracy," *Social Science History* (Winter 1997): 472. See also Theda Skocpol, Marshall Ganz and Ziad Munson, "A Nation of Joiners: The Institutional Origins of Civic Voluntarism in the United States," *The American Political Science Review* 94, no. 3 (September 2000): 17. Skocpol refers to Arthur Schlesinger, Jr.'s 1944 publication of the *Biography of a Nation of Joiners*.

18. Skocpol, "The Tocqueville Problem," 460.
19. Theda Skocpol, *Diminished Democracy: From Membership to Management in American Civic Life* (Norman: University of Oklahoma Press, 2003), 135-136, 478-490.
20. For historical analysis of the Progressives, refer to Leon Fink, *Progressive Intellectuals and the Dilemmas of Democratic Commitment* (Cambridge: Harvard University Press, 1997); Richard Hofstadter, *The Age of Reform* (New York: Vintage Books, 1955); Peter Levine, *The New Progressive Era: Toward a Fair and Deliberative Democracy* (Lanham: Rowman & Littlefield); and Michael McGerr, *A Fierce Discontent: The Rise and Fall of the Progressive Movement in America 1980 – 1920* (Oxford: Oxford University Press, 2003).
21. Levine, *The New Progressive Era*, 72; Progressive Party, "Progressive Platform of 1912," *American Progressivism: A Reader*, ed. Ronald J. Pestritto and William J. Atto (New York: Rowman & Littlefield Publishers, Inc., 2008), 273-287.
22. Hodgkinson and Foley, *The Civil Society Reader*, xviii, xxi.
23. Ibid., 23-25, 71.
24. Levine, *The New Progressive Era*, 31-32.
25. Jason Kaufman, *For the Common Good? American Civic Life and the Golden Age of Fraternity* (Oxford: Oxford University Press, 2002), 213.
26. Benjamin Barber, *Strong Democracy: Participatory Politics for a New Age* (Berkeley: University of California Press), 261.
27. Skocpol, *Diminished Democracy*, 139, 157, 180, 469.
28. Ibid., 185.
29. Jordan and Maloney, *Democracy and Interest Groups*, 87.
30. kocpol, *Diminished Democracy*, 178.
31. Knoke, "Associations and Interest Groups," 16.
32. Skocpol, *Diminished Democracy*, 158-63.
33. Ibid., 176.
34. Ibid., 191, 218-222.
35. Knoke, "Associations and Interest Groups," 2.
36. Warren, *Democracy and Association*, 10.
37. Ibid., 94.
38. Kaufman, *For the Common Good*, viii.
39. Barber, *A Place for Us*, 21. Barber provided the reference to E.E. Schattschneider's 1960 thesis.
40. Kenneth T. Andrews et al., "Leadership, Membership and Voice: Civic Associations That Work," *American Journal of Sociology* 115, no. 4 (January 2010): 1241.
41. Levine, *The New Progressive Era*, xiii, 54-57; and Skocpol, *Diminished Democracy*, 138.

42. Anne Skorkjaer Binderkrantz, "Membership Recruitment and Internal Democracy in Interest Groups: Do Group-Member Relations Vary Between Group Types?" *West European Politics* 32, no. 3 (May 2009): 657-678; and Skocpol, *Diminished Democracy,* 201-202, 220.
43. Jordan and Maloney, *Democracy and Interest Groups,* 193.
44. Ibid., 28. Jordan and Maloney quoted David B. Truman's 1951 definition.
45. Ibid., 28-30.
46. Skocpol, *Diminished Democracy,* 132-151.
47. National Center for Charitable Statistics, "National Center for Charitable Statistics: Frequently Asked Questions," http://nccs.urban.org/FAQ (accessed 3/9/11).
48. Ibid. The National Center for Charitable Statistics has concluded charitable groups received 75% of their 2008 funding from individuals, 13% from foundations, 7% in bequests and corporations.
49. Skocpol, *Diminished Democracy,* 131, 154-155.
50. National Center for Charitable Statistics, "National Center for Charitable Statistics: Frequently Asked Questions," http://nccs.urban.org/FAQ (accessed 3/9/11); and League of Women Voters, "Creating a More Perfect Union: League of Women Voters 2007-2008 Annual Report" (Washington, DC: League of Women Voters report, 2009). The other nonprofits are the American Jewish Committee (NY), a membership organization with nominal entrance fees and opportunities to participate; the Anti-Defamation League Foundation; the NRA Foundation Inc., which does not invite membership but encourages donations while the NRA parent association does seek membership at a nominal rate; the National Council of La Raza; the NAACP Legal Defense and Educational Fund, Inc., which is structured like the NRA with its parent organization accepting the members; the MS Foundation for Women, Inc.; Children's Defense Fund; Alliance Defense Fund, Inc.; and the National Women's Law Center. By manner of comparison, the civic League of Women Voters showed total revenue of $4,627,574 for fiscal year 2008.
51. Warren, *Democracy and Association,* 220-221.
52. Nancy Rosenblum, *Membership and Morals: The Personal Uses of Pluralism in America* (Princeton: Princeton University Press, 1998), 4, 17, 349.
53. Nancy Rosenblum, "The Moral Uses of Pluralism," in *Civil Society, Democracy and Civic Renewal,* ed. Robert K. Fullenwider (Lanham: Rowman & Littlefield Publishers, 1999), 270.
54. Rosenblum, *Membership and Morals,* 352.
55. Warren, "The Political Role of Non-Profits," 50.
56. Rosenblum, "The Moral Uses of Pluralism," 260.
57. Warren, "The Political Role of Non-Profits," 50.

58. Warren, *Democracy and Association,* 26, 29.
59. Rosenblum, "The Moral Uses of Pluralism," 258-259.
60. Levine, *The New Progressive Era,* 212.

Chapter 3

1. For description of these points, see Marc Hooghe, "Voluntary Associations and Socialization," in *The Handbook of Social Capital,* ed. Dario Castiglione, J W. Van Deth and Guglielmo Wolleb (Oxford: Oxford University Press, 2006), 569.
2. For description of these points, see Barber, *Strong Democracy,* 219; and Warren, *Democracy and Association,* 205.
3. Jordan and Maloney, *Democracy and Interest Groups,* 170.
4. William A. Maloney, "Interest Groups and Social Capital," in *The Handbook of Social Capital,* eds. Dario Castiglione, Jan W. Van Deth and Guglielmo Wolleb (Oxford: Oxford University Press, 2006), 310.
5. Warren, *Democracy and Association,* 61, 92, 201-202; Tocqueville, *Democracy in America,* 236.
6. Gutmann and Thompson, *Why Deliberative Democracy?,* 10-12, 27; Alison Kadlec and Will Friedman, "Deliberative Democracy and the Problem of Power" *Journal of Public Administration* 3, no. 1, art. 8 (2007), 16; and Jean Cohen, "American Civil Society Talk," in *Civil Society, Democracy and Civic Renewal,* ed. Robert K. Fullenwider (Lanham: Rowman & Littlefield Publishers, Inc.), 61-70.
7. Warren, *Democracy and Association,* 147.
8. Rosenblum, "The Moral Uses of Pluralism," 270.
9. Tocqueville, *Democracy in America,* 525.
10. Jordan and Maloney, *Democracy and Interest Groups,* 48.
11. Rosenblum, "The Moral Uses of Pluralism," 268.
12. Jordan and Maloney, *Democracy and Interest Groups,* 163.
13. Rosenblum, *Membership and Morals,* 352-353.
14. Warren, "The Political Role of Non-Profits," 46.
15. Warren, *Democracy and Association,* 171.
16. See Warren, *Democracy and Trust,* 14; William Maloney, "Interest Groups and Social Capital," 317; Robert D. Putnam, *Bowling Alone: The Collapse and Revival of American Community* (New York: Simon and Schuster, 2000); and Putnam, *Making Democracy Work: Civic Traditions in Modern Italy* (Princeton: Princeton University Press, 1993).
17. Maloney, "Interest Groups and Social Capital," 316.
18. Steven Rathgeb Smith, "Civic Infrastructure in America: The Interrelationship between Government and the Voluntary Sector," in in *Civil Society, Democracy and Civic Renewal,* ed. Robert K. Fullenwider (Lanham: Rowman & Littlefield Publishers, 1999), 136.

19. Tocqueville, *Democracy in America*, 192-95, 287.
20. For a range of negative argument, explored later in this thesis, refer to Maloney, "Interest Groups and Social Capital," in *The Handbook of Social Capital*, ed. Castiglione, Van Deth and Wolleb, 303-326; Steven N. Durlauf, "Membership and Inequality," in *The Handbook of Social Capital*, eds. Dario Castiglione, Jan W. Van Deth and Guglielmo Wolleb (Oxford: Oxford University Press, 2006), 613-614; Kaufman, *For the Common Good*, 9, 213; Jordan and Maloney, *Democracy and Interest Groups*, 18-19, 146; and Putnam, *Bowling Alone*, 160.
21. Alexander Hamilton, John Jay and James Madison, "Federalist 6," in *The Federalist Papers*, ed. Robert Scigliano (Random House: New York, 2000), 28.
22. Maloney, "Interest Groups and Social Capital," 309; and Jordan and Maloney, *Democracy and Interest Groups*, 20.
23. Jordan and Maloney, *Democracy and Interest Groups*, 20, 24.
24. Ibid., 104. The authors contend the national hunger for public negatives creates an "externality [of] increasing alienation . . . Opponents are portrayed as 'enemies' who want to destroy the values that the recipient of the mail [is] supposed to hold dear."
25. David E. Campbell, *Why We Vote: How Schools and Communities Shape Our Civic Life* (Princeton: Princeton University Press, 2006), 183; and Clarissa Hayward, "Binding Problems, Boundary Problems: the Trouble with 'Democratic Citizenship,'" in *Identities, Affiliations and Allegiances*, ed. Seyla Benhabib (Cambridge: Cambridge University Press, 2007), 181-205.
26. Melissa Williams, "Nonterritorial Boundaries of Citizenship," in *Identities, Affiliations and Allegiances*, ed. Seyla Benhabib (Cambridge: Cambridge University Press, 2007), 9.
27. Smith, "Civic Infrastructure in America," 142.
28. Knoke, "Associations and Interest Groups," 5.
29. Mancur Olson, *The Logic of Collective Action: Public Goods and the Theory of Groups* (Cambridge: Harvard University Press, 1971), 13.
30. Ibid., 33. Olson described therein David Hume's *Treatise of Human Nature*. The 1749 work addressed the challenges of caretaking common grazing ground. Considerable scholarship has been devoted to find means that overcome disincentives to public action on public problems.
31. Held, *Models of Democracy*, 232.
32. Knoke, "Associations and Interest Groups," 7-8.
33. Skocpol, *Diminished Democracy*, 142.
34. Nathan Glazer, "Reflections on Citizenship and Diversity," in *Diversity and Citizenship: Rediscovering American Nationhood*, ed. Gary Jeffrey

Jacobsohn and Susan Dunn (Lanham: Rowman & Littlefield Publishers, 1996), 85-100.

35. Jürgen Habermas, "Deliberative Politics: A Procedural Concept of Democracy" in *Between Facts and Norms: Contributions to a Discourse Theory of Law and Democracy*, trans. William Rehg (Cambridge: MIT Press, 1996), 314. Habermas references the work of Robert Dahl.

36. Gutmann and Thompson, *Why Deliberative Democracy?*, 14.

37. Barber, *A Place For Us*, 42-43.

38. Harry C. Boyte, "Building the Commonwealth: Citizenship as Public Work," in *Citizen Competence and Democratic Institutions*, ed. Steven L. Elkin and Karol Edward Soltan (University Park: Pennsylvania State University Press, 1999), 263, 269-70.

39. Jean Cohen, "Trust, Voluntary Association and Workable Democracy: The Contemporary American Discourse of Civil Society," in *Democracy and Trust*, ed. Mark E. Warren (Cambridge: Cambridge University Press, 1999), 223; Cohen, "Civil Society Talk," 70-72.

40. Theda Skocpol, Marshall Ganz and Ziad Munson, "A Nation of Organizers: The Institutional Origins of Civic Voluntarism in the United States," *The American Political Science Review* 94, no. 3 (2000), 527; Skocpol, *Diminished Democracy*, 23-57.

41. Andrews, "Leadership, Membership, and Voice," 1191.

42. Jordan and Maloney, *Democracy and Interest Groups*, 38.

43. Ibid., 38, 40.

44. Ibid., 48; R.H. Salisbury, "An Exchange Theory of Groups," *Midwest Journal of Political Science* 13, no. 1 (February 1969): 1.

45. Knoke, "Associations and Interest Groups," 2-3.

46. Warren, *Democracy and Association*, 4.

47. Warren, "The Political Role of Non-Profits, "*Society*, 48.

Chapter 4

1. Jordan and Maloney, *Democracy and Interest Groups*, 19; Maloney, "Interest Groups, Social Capital, and Democratic Politics," 309.

2. Sidney Verba, Kay Lehman Schlozman, and Henry Brady. *Voice and Equality: Civic Voluntarism in American Politics* (Cambridge: Harvard University Press, 1995), vii, 3-4, 9.

3. Kaufman, *For the Common Good?* 8; and Pamela A. Popielarz and J. Miller McPherson, "On the Edge or In Between: Niche Position, Niche Overlap, and the Duration of Voluntary Association Memberships," *The American Journal of Sociology* 101, no. 3 (November 1995): 698.

4. Binderkrantz, "Membership Recruitment and Internal Democracy in Interest Groups," 657.

5. Jordan and Maloney, *Democracy and Interest Groups*, 187.

6. Ibid., 188. Jordan and Maloney quoted Verba.
7. Maloney, "Interest Groups, Social Capital, and Democratic Politics," 312-313.
8. Salisbury, "An Exchange Theory of Groups," 1, 16.
9. John Mark Hansen, "The Political Economy of Group Membership," *The American Political Science Review* 79, no. 1 (March 1985): 79.
10. Helen P. Gouldner, "Dimensions of Organizational Commitment." *Administrative Science Quarterly* 4, 4 (March 1960): 468-469.
11. Jordan and Maloney, *Democracy and Interest Groups,* 51-53, 56.
12. Warren, *Democracy and Association,* 95-98.
13. Maloney, "Interest Groups, Social Capital, and Democratic Politics," 303-327.
14. Olson, *The Logic of Collective Action,* 5, 176-78.
15. Jordan and Maloney, *Democracy and Interest Groups,* 143. Jordan and Maloney quoted Rosenblum.
16. Ibid., 142.
17. Ibid., 144.
18. Matthew Crenson and Benjamin Ginsberg, *Downsizing Democracy: How America Sidelined its Citizens and Privatized its Public* (Baltimore: Johns Hopkins University Press, 2002), x.
19. Levine, *The New Progressive Era,* 219.

Chapter 5

1. Urban Institute/National Center for Charitable Statistics, "501(c)(3) Public Charities," http://nccsdataweb.urban.org/PubApps/nonprofit-overview-segment.php?t=pc (accessed 5/16/11). The 2009 combined income for charities was $2,623,609,530,079. The National Center for Charitable Statistics is a good source for understanding the variety among nonprofit organizations in the United States.
2. Ibid.
3. Levine, *The New Progressive Era,* 220.
4. Ibid., 57.
5. Warren, "The Political Role of Non-profits in a Democracy," 48.
6. Salisbury, "An Exchange Theory of Groups," 19-20, 31-32.
7. Levine, *The New Progressive Era,* 23.
8. Jordan and Maloney, *Democracy and Interest Groups,* 88, 114. Theda Skocpol is credited for these now widely used catch phrases.
9. Ibid., *Democracy and Interest Groups,* 33, 161-162.
10. Ibid., 161-162. Jordan and Maloney provide extensive provocative argument for the view that members may be superfluous.
11. Maloney, "Interest Groups, Social Capital, and Democratic Politics," 315. Maloney quoted Skocpol.
12. Kaufman, *For the Common Good,* 6.

13. Andrews, "Leadership, Membership, and Voice: Civic Associations That Work," 1198-1202.
14. Ibid., 1191-1192.
15. Skocpol, Ganz and Munson, "A Nation of Organizers," 10-11.
16. Salisbury, "An Exchange Theory of Groups," 15.
17. Jordan and Maloney, *Democracy and Interest Groups*, 91. The book features the writing efforts of Gregory Dees, Jed Emerson and Peter Economy.
18. Andrews, "Leadership, Membership, and Voice," 1191.
19. Knoke, "Associations and Interest Groups," 10.
20. Jordan and Maloney, *Democracy and Interest Groups*, 91; and League of Women Voters, "Audited Consolidated Financial Statements and Other Financial Information, League of Voters, June 30, 2009" (Washington, DC: League of Women Voters financial statement, 2010).
21. Jordan and Maloney, *Democracy and Interest Groups*, 86, 90-91.
22. Ibid., 100-101.
23. Ibid., 100-101.
24. Maloney, "Interest Groups, Social Capital, and Democratic Politics," 320. Maloney referred to Verba, Schlozman and Brady's position.
25. Jordan and Maloney, *Democracy and Interest Groups*, 100.
26. Ibid., 91.
27. Knoke, "Associations and Interest Groups," 12.
28. Andrews, "Leadership, Membership, and Voice," 1191-1192.
29. Levine, *The New Progressive Era*, 220.
30. John D. McCarthy, "Persistence and Change Among Nationally-Federated Social Movements," in *Social Movements and Organization Theory*, ed. Gerald F. Davis et al. (New York: Cambridge University Press, 2005), 193.
31. Jordan and Maloney, *Democracy and Interest Groups*, 88-89; ABC News, http://abcnews.go.com/GMA/Weekend/story?id=6258425 (accessed 4/8/11).
32. Jordan and Maloney, *Democracy and Interest Groups*, 107.
33. Ibid., 123; and Salisbury, "An Exchange Theory of Groups," 31-32.
34. Jordan and Maloney, *Democracy and Interest Groups*, 119.
35. Levine, *The New Progressive Era*, 221.
36. Maloney, "Interest Groups, Social Capital, and Democratic Politics," 311-313.
37. Putnam, *Bowling Alone*, 27-28; and Cohen, "American Civil Society Talk," 79.
38. Skocpol, *Diminished Democracy*, 127.
39. Michael Schudson, *The Good Citizen: A History of American Civic Life* (Cambridge: Harvard University Press, 1999), 310.

40. Putnam, *Bowling Alone,* 160.
41. Levine, *The New Progressive Era,* 211-212.
42. Skocpol, *Diminished Democracy,* 222-223, 231, 238.
43. Levine, *The New Progressive Era,* 58; Putnam, *Bowling Alone,* 31-47.
44. Skocpol, *Diminished Democracy,* 191, 242.
45. Warren, *Democracy and Association,* 211.
46. Skocpol, *Diminished Democracy,* 259.
47. Ibid., 280, 282-83, 280.
48. Levine, *The New Progressive Era,* 212-213.

Chapter 6

1. Warren, *Democracy and Association,* 149.
2. Karen J. Blair, "Introduction" in "Special Issue on Women's Clubs," *Frontiers: A Journal of Women Studies* 30, no. 3 (2009): x. This Blair phrase first appears in the title of this chapter and is also alluded to in Chapter 7's heading.
3. Alexander Keyssar, *The Right to Vote: The Contested History of Democracy in the United States* (New York: Basic Books, 2000), xxi.
4. Gail Collins, "My Favorite August," *The New York Times,* August 13, 2010.
5. Robert P.J. Cooney, *Winning the Vote: The Triumph of the American Woman Suffrage Movement* (Santa Cruz: American Graphic Press, 2005), xiv.
6. Louise Young, *In the Public Interest: The League of Women Voters 1920 – 1970 (Contributions in American Studies)* (Westport: Greenwood Press, 1989), 8-15.
7. Michael McGerr, "Political Style and Women's Power, 1830 – 1930," *The Journal of American History* 77, no. 3 (December 1990): 864-885; and Costain, "Representing Women," 100-113.
8. Barbara Stuhler, *For the Public Record: A Documentary History of the League of Women Voters* (Westport: Greenwood Press, 2000), 22.
9. Young, *In the Public Interest,* 33. Catt later judged compulsory civic education unnecessary.
10. Marilyn Gittell and Teresa Shtob, "Changing Women's Roles in Political Volunteerism and Reform of the City" in "Supplement on Women and the American City," *Signs* 5, no. 3 (Spring 1980): S67-S78.
11. Lynn Dumenil, "The New Woman and the Politics of the 1920s," *OAH Magazine of History* 21, no. 3 (July 2007): 24. See also Anne N. Costain, "Representing Women: The Transition from Social Movement to Interest Group" in "Special Issue on Women and Politics," *The Western Political Quarterly* 34, no. 1 (March 1981): 100-104.
12. Cooney, *Winning the Vote,* 436.

13. Sara Alpern and Dale Baum, "Female Ballots: The Impact of the Nine-teenth Amendment," *Journal of Interdisciplinary History* 16, no. 1 (Summer 1985): 46, 56-57; Kristi Anderson, *After Suffrage: Women in Partisan and Electoral Politics Before the New Deal* (Chicago: The University of Chicago Press, 1996), 1, 7-28, 95-105; and Young, *In the Public Interest*, 2.

14. Alpern and Baum, "Female Ballots," 43.

15. Ibid., 61, 63.

16. For membership figures through the 1920s, see Young, *In the Public Interest*, 153; and Stuhler, *For the Public Record*, 249.

17. Stuhler, *For the Public Record*, 33. Italics added.

18. Anderson, *After Suffrage*, 46-50; and Keyssar, *The Right to Vote*, 224-243.

19. Linda Damaris Sayre, "Volunteer Leaders: Learning and Development in the League of Women Voters," Ph.D. preview (New Brunswick: Rutgers The State University of New Jersey, 2002), 3.

20. Cooney, *Winning the Vote*, 451; Dumenil, "The New Woman and the Politics of the 1920s," 25; and Young, *In the Public Interest*, 169.

21. Young, *In the Public Interest*, 110.

22. Michael McGerr, "Political Style and Women's Power, 1830-1930," *The Journal of American History* 77, no. 3 (December 1990), 873-874, 879.

23. Young, *In the Public Interest*, 33, 38; Kay J. Maxwell, "The League of Women Voters Through the Decades" (Washington, DC: League of Women Voters booklet, 2007), 3.

24. James G. Hougland Jr. and James R. Wood, "Control in Organizations and the Commitment of Members," *Social Forces* 59, no. 1 (September 1980): 85-88.

25. Young, *In the Public Interest*, 67-69; and Hilda R. Watrous, "In League with Eleanor: Eleanor Roosevelt and the League of Women Voters, 1921 – 1962" (New York: League of Women Voters of New York State booklet, 1984), 93.

26. Young, *In the Public Interest*, 1; and Sayre, "Volunteer Leaders," 10.

27. Young, *In the Public Interest*, 1.

28. Ibid., 155.

29. League of Women Voters, "League Basics" (Washington, DC: League of Women Voters booklet, 2009), 3, 7, 12.

30. The mission statement is recorded in Sayre, "Volunteer Leaders," 2.

31. Fink, *Progressive Intellectuals and the Dilemmas of Democratic Commitment*, 15, 23.

32. McGerr, "Political Style and Women's Power, 1830-1930," 864-885.

33. Dumenil, "The New Woman and the Politics of the 1920s," 241; and Hilda R. Watrous, "In League with Eleanor: Eleanor Roosevelt and the League of Women Voters, 1921–1962 (New York: League of Women Voters of New York State booklet, 1984), 3.

34. Watrous, "In League with Eleanor," 3.
35. Young, *In the Public Interest,* 40.
36. Young, *In the Public Interest,* 84-143; and Watrous, "In League with Eleanor."
37. Anderson, *After Suffrage,* 36.
38. Ibid., 35, 44.
39. Verba, Schlozman, and Brady, *Voice and Equality,* vii, 3-4, 9.
40. Young, *In the Public Interest,* 2.
41. Fink, *Progressive Intellectuals and the Dilemmas of Democratic Commitment,* 28-31. Indeed, Carrie Chapman Catt would consider willful twisting of the public sphere to have been the primary impediment of women's suffrage.
42. Cooney, Jr. *Winning the Vote,* 383.
43. Stuhler, *For the Public Record,* 287.
44. Cooney, *Winning the Vote,* 447.
45. Liette Patricia Gidlow, Ph.D., "Getting Out the Vote: Gender and Citizenship in an Age of Consumer Culture," Ph.D. abstract summary (Ithaca: Cornell University, 1997).
46. Anderson, *After Suffrage,* 35.
47. Dumenil, "The New Woman and the Politics of the 1920s," 879, 885.
48. For a description of this gradual transition, refer to Cooney, *Winning the Vote*; Costain, "Representing Women," 100-113; Christine A. Lunardini and Thomas J. Knock, "Woodrow Wilson and Woman Suffrage," *Political Science Quarterly* 95, no. 4 (Winter 1980-1981): 655-671; McGerr, "Political Style and Women's Power, 1870 – 1920," 864-885; and Keyssar, *The Right to Vote.*
49. Young, *In the Public Interest,* 20.
50. Ibid., 27.
51. Roberta Francis, "Changed Forever: The League of Women Voters and the Equal Rights Amendment" (Washington, DC: League of Women Voters Education Fund booklet, 1988), 35.
52. Warner Olivier, "The League of Frightened Women," *Saturday Evening Post* 227, no. 17 (October 23, 1954): 32.
53. Olivier, "The League of Frightened Women," 98; and *The DC Voter: A Voice for Citizens, A Force for Change* 86, no. 9 (November 2010), 6.
54. Karen J. Blair, "Introduction" in "Special Issue on Women's Clubs," ix.
55. Melissa Estes Blair, "A Dynamic Force in Our Community: Women's Clubs and Second-Wave Feminism at the Grassroots," in "Special Issue on Women's Clubs," *Frontiers: A Journal of Women Studies* 30, no. 3 (2009): 32-33.
56. Karen J. Blair, "Introduction" in "Special Issue on Women's Clubs," x. Blair's point is in reference to Melissa Estes Blair's research.

57. Melissa Estes Blair, "A Dynamic Force in Our Community," 39-40.
58. Olivier, "The League of Frightened Women," 102. Italics added.
59. Young, *In the Public Interest*, 75.
60. Olivier, "The League of Frightened Women," 102.
61. Marisa Chappell, "Rethinking Women's Politics in the 1970s: The League of Women Voters and the National Organization for Women Confront Poverty," *Journal of Women's History* 13, no. 4 (Winter 2002): 165.
62. Young, *In the Public Interest*, 20, 45.
63. Sayre, "Volunteer Leaders," 5.
64. Stuhler, *For the Public Record*, 292.
65. Young, *In the Public Interest*, 64, 82.
66. Stuhler, *For the Public Record*, 220.
67. Young, *In the Public Interest*.
68. Stuhler, *For the Public Record*, 244; Young, *In the Public Interest*, 82.
69. Maxwell, "The League of Women Voters Through the Decades," 2.
70. Sayre, "Volunteer Leaders," 27. Italics added.
71. Kadlec and Friedman, "Deliberative Democracy and the Problem of Power."
72. Stuhler, *For the Public Record*, viii-xiv.
73. Fink, *Progressive Intellectuals and the Dilemmas of Democratic Commitment*, 18. Italics added.
74. Gloria Feldt, *No Excuses: Nine Ways Women Can Change How We Think About Power* (Berkeley: Seal Press, 2010), 38.
75. Sayre, "Volunteer Leaders," 13, 33.
76. League of Women Voters, "League Basics," 32.
77. League of Women Voters, "League Basics," 22; and League of Women Voters, "Creating a More Perfect Union."
78. Sayre, "Volunteer Leaders," 13; and Olivier, "The League of Frightened Women," 101.
79. Hansen, "The Political Economy of Group Membership," 88, 90.
80. Salisbury, "An Exchange Theory of Groups," 1-32.
81. Young, *In the Public Interest*, 15, 76.
82. For information on Eleanor Roosevelt's rich engagement with the League of Women Voters, refer to Watrous, "In League with Eleanor."
83. Rod Clare, "Resisting 'the Doldrums': The League of Women Voters in North Carolina in the 1950s," *North Carolina Historical Review* 86, no. 2 (April 2009): 181.
84. Genevieve B. Earle recounted her civic convictions experienced through the Brooklyn branch of the League of Women Voters on *The Bob Edward Show*. Genevieve B. Earle, interview by Bob Edward, This I Believe Collection, National Public Radio, Washington, DC, Feb-

ruary 19, 2010. See http://thisibelieve.org/essay/16524/ (accessed on 10/11/10).

85. Sayre, "Volunteer Leaders," 10.
86. Young, *In the Public Interest*, 155.
87. Helen P. Gouldner, "Dimensions of Organizational Commitment," *Administrative Science Quarterly* 4, no. 4 (March 1960): 472.
88. Melissa Estes Blair, "A Dynamic Force in Our Community," 30. (Italics added.)
89. Skocpol, *Diminished Democracy*, 154-55.
90. Young, *In the Public Interest*, 156-57.
91. Gittell and Shtob, "Changing Women's Roles in Political Volunteerism and Reform of the City," S77.
92. Stuhler, *For the Public Record*, 289; and Costain, "Representing Women," 108-109.
93. Hansen, "The Political Economy of Group Membership," 89.
94. Peter Levine, *The New Progressive Era*, 58.
95. Stuhler, *For the Public Record*, i-vii; and League of Women Voters, "League Basics," 3.
96. Recorded within the League's member section under "League Story-bank." See http://www.lwv.org (accessed 9/15/11).
97. Anne N. Costain, "The Struggle for a National Women's Lobby: Organizing a Diffuse Interest," *The Western Political Quarterly* 33, no. 4 (December 1980): 484-486; David Vogel, "The Public Interest Movement and the American Reform Tradition," *Political Science Quarterly* 95, no. 4 (Winter 1980-1981), 614.
98. Sayre, "Volunteer Leaders," 6.
99. Young, *In the Public Interest*, 75.
100. Sayre, "Volunteer Leaders," 6.
101. See http://www.nyfera.org/?p=3161 (accessed 2/17/11).
102. For information on membership shifts, refer to Sayre, "Volunteer Leaders," 9-10; Young, *In the Public Interest*, 148, 153, 179; Stuhler, *For the Public Record*, 247-249, 264, 271, 289; and Chappell, "Rethinking Women's Politics in the 1970s," 157.
103. Olivier, "The League of Frightened Women," 33.
104. Stuhler, *For the Public Record*, 247, 264.
105. Clare, "Resisting 'the Doldrums,'" 201-207.
106. Maxwell, "The League of Women Voters Through the Decades," 5.
107. Stuhler, *For the Public Record*, 247.
108. Ibid., 265-289. (Italics added.)
109. Francis, "Changed Forever," 25.
110. Costain, "The Struggle for a National Women's Lobby," 483.
111. Nancy Tate, interview by author, Washington, DC, May 20, 2011.

112. League of Women Voters, "Opening Doors to Democracy: League of Women Voters 2008-2009 Annual Report" (Washington, DC: League of Women Voters Report, 2010); also http://www.lwv.org (accessed 9/15/11).
113. Maxwell, "The League of Women Voters Through the Decades," 6.
114. League of Women Voters, "Opening Doors to Democracy: League of Women Voters 2008-2009 Annual Report" (Washington, DC: League of Women Voters report, 2010).
115. League of Women Voters, "Creating a More Perfect Union: League of Women Voters 2007-2008 Annual Report."
116. Andrews, "Leadership, Membership, and Voice;" and http://www.lwv.org (accessed 5/10/11).
117. Sayre, "Volunteer Leaders," 10.
118. League of Women Voters, "Creating a More Perfect Union: League of Women Voters 2007-2008 Annual Report."
119. League of Women Voters, "Opening Doors to Democracy: League of Women Voters 2008-2009 Annual Report."
120. Warren, *Democracy and Association*, 164; "Capital Research Group," http://www.capitalresearch.org/news/news.html?id=431(accessed 2/17/11); and http://www.lwv.org (accessed 9/15/11).
121. See "President's Handbook: Financial Guidelines" issued on August 2010 by the LWV of Illinois Education Fund, accessed through http://www.lwvil.org (accessed 9/17/11).
122. "Centre" and "Jefferson" 2009 figures are derived from the National Center for Charitable Statistics. See http://nccsdataweb.urban.org/PubApps/search.php (accessed 2/17/11). See "League of Women Voters of the District of Columbia Proposed Budget 2011-2012," as submitted to the LWVDC Annual meeting on April 16, 2011.
123. See "League of Women Voters of the District of Columbia Proposed Budget 2011-2012."
124. Stuhler, *For the Public Record;* League of Women Voters, "Opening Doors to Democracy: League of Women Voters 2008-2009 Annual Report;" and http://www.lwv.org (accessed 9/15/11).
125. League of Women Voters, "League Basics," 11.

Chapter 7

1. Acknowledgments of this sentiment by Mark E. Warren, Robert D. Putnam, John Mark Hansen and Michael Schudson are cited in earlier sections of this work.
2. Warren, *Democracy and Association*, 149.
3. A line rendered by fiction writer Mary Travers' Mary Poppins, in regard to her own character, within the Disney movie carrying her name. See www.imdb.com/title/tt0058331/quotes (accessed 6/26/12).

4. Warren, *Democracy and Association*, 214-215. Warren draws from Nancy Rosenblum's description of democratic influence on daily life.
5. Jordan and Maloney, *Democracy and Interest* Groups, 187. Jordan and Maloney reference the work of Sidney Verba.
6. Olivier, "The League of Frightened Women," 101.
7. Gittell and Shtob, "Changing Women's Roles in Political Volunteerism and Reform of the City," S74.
8. Stuhler, *For the Public Record*, 57.
9. Cooney, Jr., *Winning the Vote*, 420; and Sayre, "Volunteer Leaders, 10.
10. Warren, *Democracy and Association*, 160.
11. Sayre, "Volunteer Leaders," v; and Francis, "Changed Forever," 37.
12. Sayre, "Volunteer Leaders," v.
13. Terrianne K. Schulte, "Citizen Experts: The League of Women Voters and Environmental Conservation" in "Special Issue on Women's Clubs," *Frontiers: A Journal of Women Studies* 30, no. 3 (2009): 3.
14. Gouldner, "Dimensions of Organizational Commitment," 469.
15. Held, *Models of Democracy*, 223. Held describes "democratic" versus "liberal" orientations toward democracy.
16. Salisbury, "An Exchange Theory of Groups," 16.
17. Hansen, "The Political Economy of Group Membership," 88.
18. Gittell and Shtob, "Changing Women's Roles in Political Volunteerism and Reform of the City," S77.
19. Warren, *Democracy and Association*, 208.
20. James G. Hougland, Jr. and James R. Wood, "Control in Organizations and the Commitment of Members," *Social Forces* 59, no. 1 (September 1980): 313; and Jordan and Maloney, *Democracy and Interest Groups*, 176.
21. Vogel, "The Public Interest Movement and the American Reform Tradition," 625.
22. Matt Leighninger, "Is Everything Up to Date in Kansas City? Why 'Citizen Involvement' May Soon Be Obsolete," *National Civic Review* (Summer 2007): 13.
23. Schulte, "Citizen Experts," 4.
24. Keyssar, *The Right to Vote*, 175.
25. "The Republican Threat to Voting," *New York Times*, April 26, 2011; and "Study: Voting Laws Will Change 2012 Landscape," *Washington Post*, October 4, 2011.
26. David W. Ogden, "League of Women Voters (LWV), Amicus Curiae," *Supreme Court Debates* 9, no. 4 (April 2006), 122.
27. Young, *In the Public Interest*, 93-100. Further documentation is bountiful through League websites and archives.
28. Maxwell, "The League of Women Voters Through the Decades," 3.

29. League of Women Voters, "Creating a More Perfect Union: League of Women Voters 2007-2008 Annual Report."
30. Young, *In the Public Interest*, 3.
31. Anderson, *After Suffrage*, 105; and Michael McGrath, "Progressive Passion: Reviving the Fighting Spirit of Nonpartisan Reform," *National Civic Review* (Fall 2005): 21.
32. Kathleen Hale and Ramona McNeal, "Election Administration Reform and State Choice: Voter Identification Requirements and HAVA," *Policy Studies Journal* 38, no. 2 (May 2010), 281.
33. "The Republican Threat to Voting," *New York Times*, April 26, 2011. See also "Study: Voting Laws Will Change 2012 Landscape," *Washington Post*, October 4, 2011.
34. Vogel, "The Public Interest and the American Reform Tradition," 610-611.
35. See, for example, Ogden, "League of Women Voters (LWV), Amicus Curiae," 122.
36. See http://www.lwvdc.org (accessed 9/15/11).
37. Schulte, "Citizen Experts," 2.
38. Ibid., 18.
39. League of Women Voters, "Creating a More Perfect Union: League of Women Voters 2007-2008 Annual Report."
40. See http://www.lwv.org (accessed 9/15/11).
41. James Mattingly, "How to Become Your Own Worst Adversary: Examining the Connection Between Managerial Attributions and Organizational Relationships with Public Interest Stakeholders," *Journal of Public Affairs* 7 (2007): 8.
42. See, for example, http://www.arlnow.com/2010/06/22/league-of-women-voters-in-dust-up-with-committee-for-a-better-arlington/ (accessed 9/3/11).
43. Gutmann and Thompson, *Why Deliberative Democracy?*, 48. Italics added.
44. Chappell, "Rethinking Women's Politics in the 1970s," 157.
45. Young, *In the Public Interest*, 54.
46. League of Women Voters, "Where We Stand: Position Statement of the LWV of the District of Columbia" (Washington, DC: League of Women Voters of the District of Columbia brochure, 2009).
47. Costain, "Representing Women," 109-110.
48. League of Women Voters, *The League Voice: Making a Difference in Your Community* (September 2011).
49. Costain, "The Struggle for a National Women's Lobby," 479.
50. Vogel, "The Public Interest Movement and the American Reform Tradition," 614; and Costain, "The Struggle for a National Women's Lobby," 486.

51. Francis, "Changed Forever," 39-40.
52. Young, *In the Public Interest*, 49.
53. Clare, "Resisting 'the Doldrums,'" 201.
54. Vogel, "The Public Interest Movement and the American Reform Tradition," 610.
55. See, for example, Megan Threlkeld, "The Pan American Conference of Women, 1922: Successful Suffragists Turn to International Relations," *Diplomatic History* 31, no. 5 (November 2007): 801-828.
56. Schulte, "Citizen Experts," 22.
57. Francis, "Changed Forever," 37.
58. Maxwell, "The League of Women Voters Through the Decades," 5.
59. Schulte, "Citizen Experts," 1-29.
60. Ibid., 58.
61. Shklar, *American Citizenship*, 2-3; and "Study: Voting Laws Will Change 2012 Landscape," *New York Times*, October 4, 2011.
62. Vogel, "The Public Interest Movement and the American Reform Tradition," 626.
63. Francis, "Changed Forever," 14, 24, 32.
64. Warren, *Democracy and Association*, 149.
65. Ibid., 149.
66. Campbell, *Why We Vote*, 183.
67. Sayre, "Volunteer Leaders," 4.
68. Schulte, "Citizen Experts," 5.
69. Sayre, "Volunteer Leaders," 4.
70. Stuhler, *For the Public Record*, 70.
71. See "Some Republican Lawmakers Rewriting State Election Laws: Democrats at Risk," in *Washington Post*, September 16, 2011.
72. Levine, *The New Progressive Era*, 212-213.
73. Nancy Tate, interview by author, Washington, DC, May 20, 2011.
74. Ibid., 8.
75. Paul Pierson and Theda Skocpol, *The Transformation of American Politics: Activist Government and the Rise of Conservatism* (Princeton: Princeton University Press, 2007), 2-3.
76. Nancy Tate, interview by author, Washington, DC, May 20, 2011.
77. Putnam, *Bowling Alone*, 156.

Chapter 8

1. Gutmann and Thompson, *Why Deliberative Democracy?*, 149.
2. Vogel, "The Public Interest Movement and the American Reform Tradition," 626.
3. League of Women Voters of Oregon, "Membership Committee Report," January 31, 2011. https://lwvor.wordpress.com/past-events-

and-docs/all-2011-convention/latest-new/membership-committee-report/. (Accessed 9/17/11.)

4. McGrath, "Progressive Passion, 21.
5. Gutmann and Thompson, *Why Deliberative Democracy?*, 115.
6. Habermas, "Deliberative Politics," 314. Habermas quotes Robert Dahl.
7. Warren, "The Political Role of Non-Profits," 48.
8. Hansen, "The Political Economy of Group Membership," 90.
9. Schulte, "Citizen Experts," 1-29.
10. Cooney, Jr., *Winning the Vote*, 436.
11. Gutmann and Thompson, *Why Deliberative Democracy?*, 89.
12. Ibid., 51.
13. Young, *In the Public Interest*, 82.
14. Gutmann and Thompson, *Why Deliberative Democracy?*, 142.
15. Sayre, "Volunteer Leaders," 27.
16. Jordan and Maloney, *Democracy and Interest Groups, 116-162.*
17. Vogel, "The Public Interest Movement and the American Reform Tradition," 627.
18. Rosenblum, *Membership and Morals,* 4, 17, 349.
19. Clare, "Resisting 'the Doldrums,'" 184.
20. Habermas, "Deliberative Politics," 300.
21. Pierson and Skocpol, *The Transformation of American Politics*, 2-3.
22. Shklar, *American Citizenship*, 2-3.
23. Pierson and Skocpol, *The Transformation of American Politics,* 65.
24. Habermas, "Deliberative Politics," 198.
25. Ibid., 233.
26. For information on League of Women Voters membership shifts, refer to Sayre, "Volunteer Leaders," 148, 153. 179; Stuhler, *For the Public Record*, 247-249, 264, 271, 289; and Chappell, "Rethinking Women's Politics in the 1970s," 157. For information on membership shifts within the General Federation of Women's Clubs membership, refer to Skocpol, *Diminished Democracy*, 91, 130-131, 154-155, 162; and http://www.gfwc.org (accessed 9/17/11). For information on the National Society Daughters of the American Revolution, see National Society Daughters of the American Revolution, "Official Membership Count [1892 – 1996]" (Washington, DC: National Society Daughters of the American Revolution, 1996); and http://www.dar.org (accessed 9/19/11). U.S. population figures are drawn from http://www.Quickfacts.census.gov.qfd/states/00000.html and http://www.npg.org/facts/us_historical_pops.htm (accessed 9/12/11).
27. For information on League of Women Voters membership shifts, refer to Sayre, "Volunteer Leaders, 148, 153. 179; Stuhler, *For the Public Record*, 247-249, 264, 271, 289; and Chappell, "Rethinking Women's Poli-

tics in the 1970s," 157. U.S. population figures are drawn from http://www.Quickfacts.census.gov.qfd/states/00000.html and http://www.npg.org/facts/us_historical_pops.htm (accessed 9/12/11).
28. Nancy Tate, interview by author, Washington, DC, May 20, 2011.

Bibliography

Alpern, Sara, and Dale Baum. "Female Ballots: The Impact of the Nineteenth Amendment." *Journal of Interdisciplinary History* 16, no. 1 (Summer 1985): 43-67. http://www.jstor.org/stable/204321 (accessed 10/28/2010).

Andersen, Kristi. *After Suffrage: Women in Partisan and Electoral Politics Before the New Deal.* Chicago: The University of Chicago Press, 1996.

Andrews, Kenneth T. et al. "Leadership, Membership, and Voice: Civic Associations That Work." *American Journal of Sociology* 115, no. 4 (January 2010): 1191-1242. http://www.journals.uchicago.edu.library.lausys.georgetown.edu/doi/pdf/10.1086/649060 (accessed 11/19/10).

Arneil, Barbara. *Diverse Communities: The Problem with Social Capital.* Cambridge: Cambridge University Press, 2006.

Barber, Benjamin. *Strong Democracy: Participatory Politics for a New Age.* Berkeley: University of California Press, 2003.

_____. *A Place for Us: How to Make Society Civil and Democracy Strong.* New York: Hill and Wang, 1998.

Bellah, Robert N. et al. *Habits of the Heart: Individualism and Commitment in American Life.* 2nd ed. Berkeley: University of California Press, 1996.

Benhabib, Seyla, ed. *Identities, Affiliations, and Allegiances.* Cambridge: Cambridge University Press, 2007.

Binderkrantz, Anne Skorkjaer. "Membership Recruitment and Internal Democracy in Interest Groups: Do Group-Membership Relations Vary Between Group Types?" *West European Politics* 32, no. 3 (May 2009): 657-678.

Blair, Karen J. "Introduction." In "Special Issue on Women's Clubs," *Frontiers: A Journal of Women Studies* 30, no. 3 (2009): ix-xi. http://search.ebscohost.com/login.aspx?direct=true&db=aph&AN=47903353&site=ehost-live (accessed 9/16/10).

Blair, Melissa Estes. "A Dynamic Force in Our Community: Women's Clubs and Second-Wave Feminism at the Grassroots." In "Special Issue on Women's Clubs," *Frontiers: A Journal of Women Studies* 30, no. 3 (2009): 30-51. http://search.ebscohost.com/login.aspx?direct=true&db=aph&AN=47903355&site=ehost-live (accessed 9/16/10).

Boucher, Toni, and Stephen Hudspeth. "Ethics and the Nonprofit." Wilton: Common Fund Institute booklet, 2008.

Campbell, David E. *Why We Vote: How Schools and Communities Shape Our Civic Life*. Princeton: Princeton University Press, 2006.

Castiglione, Dario, Jan W. Van Deth and Guglielmo Wolleb, eds. *The Handbook of Social Capital*. Oxford: Oxford University Press, 2008.

Catt, Carrie Chapman. "Con: Should Congress Approve the Proposed Equal Rights Amendment to the Constitution?" *Congressional Digest* 22, no. 4 (April 1943): 118-128. http://search.ebscohost.com/login.aspx?direct=true&db=aph&AN=11901736&site=ehost-live (accessed 9/16/10).

Chappell, Marisa. "Rethinking Women's Politics in the 1970s: The League of Women Voters and the National Organization for Women Confront Poverty." *Journal of Women's History* 13, no. 4 (Winter 2002): 155-179. http://search.ebsco.com/login.aspx&direct=true&db=aph&AN=5881172&site=ehost-live (accessed 9/20/10).

Clare, Rod. "Resisting 'the Doldrums': The League of Women Voters in North Carolina in the 1950s." *North Carolina Historical Review* 86, no. 2 (April 2009): 180-207. http://search.ebscohost.com/login.aspx?direct=true&db=aph&AN=41129269&site=ehost=live (accessed 9/16/10).

Cooney, Jr., Robert P.J. *Winning the Vote: The Triumph of the American Woman Suffrage Movement*. Santa Cruz: American Graphic Press, 2005.

Costain, Anne N. "Representing Women: The Transition from Social Movement to Interest Group." In "Special Issue on Women and Politics," *The Western Political Quarterly* 34, no. 1, (March 1981): 100-113. http://www.jstor.org/stable/447893 (accessed 10/28/10).

_____. "The Struggle for a National Women's Lobby: Organizing a Diffuse Interest." *The Western Political Quarterly* 33, No. 4 (December 1980): 476-491. http://www.jstor.org/stable/448066 (accessed 10/28/10).

Crenson, Matthew, and Benjamin Ginsberg. *Downsizing Democracy: How America Sidelined Its Citizens and Privatized its Public*. Baltimore: Johns Hopkins University Press, 2002.

Dewey, John. *The Essential Dewey: Volume I, Pragmatism, Education, Democracy*. Edited by Larry A. Hickman and Thomas M. Alexander. Bloomington: Indiana University Press, 1998.

Dumenil, Lynn. "The New Woman and the Politics of the 1920s." *OAH Magazine of History* 21, no. 3 (July 2007): 22-26. http://search.ebscohost.

com/login.aspx?direct=true&db=aph&AN=26162961&site=ehost-live (accessed 9/16/10).

Elkin, Stephen L., and Karol Edward Soltan, eds. *Citizen Competence and Democratic Institutions*. University Park: Pennsylvania State University Press, 1999.

Elliott, Carolyn, ed. *Civil Society and Democracy: A Reader*. New Delhi: Oxford University Press, 2003.

Feldt, Gloria. *No Excuses: Nine Ways Women Can Change How We Think About Power*. Berkeley: Seal Press, 2010.

Fink, Leon. *Progressive Intellectuals and the Dilemmas of Democratic Commitment*. Cambridge: Harvard University Press, 1997.

Francis, Roberta. "Changed Forever: The League of Women Voters and the Equal Rights Amendment." Washington, DC: League of Women Voters Education Fund, 1988.

Fullenwider, Robert K., ed. *Civil Society, Democracy, and Civic Renewal*. Lanham: Rowman & Littlefield Publishers, 1999.

Gidlow, Liette Patricia. "Getting Out the Vote: Gender and Citizenship in an Age of Consumer Culture." Ph.D. abstract summary. Ithaca: Cornell University, 1997.

Gittell, Marilyn, and Teresa Shtob. "Changing Women's Roles in Political Volunteerism and Reform of the City." In "Supplement Women and the American City," *Signs* 5, no. 3 (Spring 1980): S67-S78. http://www.jstor.org/stable/3173807 (accessed 10/28/10).

Gouldner, Helen P. "Dimensions of Organizational Commitment." *Administrative Science Quarterly* 4, no. 4 (March 1960): 468-490. http://www.jstor.org/stable/2390769 (accessed 10/28/10).

Gutmann, Amy and Dennis Thompson. *Why Deliberative Democracy?* Princeton: Princeton University Press, 2004.

Habermas, Jürgen. *Between Facts and Norms: Contributions to a Discourse Theory of Law and Democracy*. Translated by William Rehg. Cambridge: MIT Press, 1996.

Hale, Kathleen and Ramona McNeal. "Election Administration Reform and State Choice: Voter Identification Requirements and HAVA." *Policy Studies Journal* 38, no. 2 (May 2010): 281-302. http://proquest.umi.com/pqdweb?did=2034999951&Fmt=3&clientld=5604&RQT=309&VName=PQD (accessed on 5/10/11).

Hamilton, Alexander, John Jay and James Madison. *The Federalist Papers*. Edited by Robert Scigliano. Random House: New York, 2000.

Hansen, John Mark. "The Political Economy of Group Membership." *The American Political Science Review* 79, no. 1 (March 1985): 79-96. http://www.jstor.org/stable/1956120 (accessed 10/27/10).

Held, David. *Models of Democracy*. Stanford: Stanford University Press, 2006.

Hodgkinson, Virginia A., and Michael W. Foley, eds. *The Civil Society Reader*. Hanover: University Press of New England, 2003.

Hofstadter, Richard. *The Age of Reform*. New York: Vintage Books, 1955.

Hougland, Jr., James G., and James R. Wood. "Control in Organizations and the Commitment of Members." *Social Forces* 59, no. 1 (September 1980): 85-105. http://catalog.library.georgetown.edu/webbridge ~S4/showresource?returnurl=%2Fsearch~S4%3F%2FX%28Social%252OF orces%29%26searchschope%3D4%26SORT%3DD%26terms%3D (accessed 11/19/10).

Jacobsohn, Gary Jeffrey, and Susan Dunn. *Diversity and Citizenship: Rediscovering American Nationhood*. Lanham: Rowman & Littlefield Publishers, Inc., 1996.

Jordan, Grant, and William A. Maloney. *Democracy and Interest Groups: Enhancing Participation?* New York: Palgrave Macmillan, 2007.

Kadlec, Alison, and Will Friedman. "Deliberative Democracy and the Problem of Power." *Journal of Public Administration* 3, no. 1, art. 8 (2007). http://www.auburn.edu/academic/liberal_arts/poli_sci/journal_public_deliberation/ (accessed 11/19/10).

Kaufman, Jason. *For the Common Good? American Civic Life and the Golden Age of Fraternity*. Oxford: Oxford University Press, 2002.

Keyssar, Alexander. *The Right to Vote: The Contested History of Democracy in the United States*. New York: Basic Books, 2000.

Knoke, David. "Associations and Interest Groups." *Annual Review of Sociology* 12 (1986): 1-21. http://www.jstor.org/stable/2083192 (accessed 10/14/10).

League of Women Voters. "Creating a More Perfect Union: League of Women Voters 2007-2008 Annual Report." Washington, DC: League of Women Voters report, 2009.

_____. "League Basics." Washington, DC: League of Women Voters booklet, 2009.

_____. "Opening Doors to Democracy: League of Women Voters 2008-2009 Annual Report." Washington, DC: League of Women Voters report, 2010.

League of Women Voters of the District of Columbia. "Where We Stand: Position Statements of the League of Women Voters of the District of Columbia." Washington, DC: League of Women Voters brochure, June 2009.

Leighninger, Matt. "Is Everything Up to Date in Kansas City? Why 'Citizen Involvement' May Soon Be Obsolete." *National Civic Review* (Summer 2007): 12-27. http://www.interscience.wiley.com (accessed 10/14/10).

Levine, Peter. *The Future of Democracy: Developing the Next Generation of American Citizens*. Medford: Tufts University Press, 2007.

_____. *The New Progressive Era: Toward a Fair and Deliberative Democracy.* Lanham: Rowman & Littlefield, 2000.

Lunardini, Christine A., and Thomas J. Knock. "Woodrow Wilson and Woman Suffrage." *Political Science Quarterly* 95, no. 4 (Winter 1980-1981): 655-671. http://www.jstor.org/stable/2150609 (accessed 9/13/10).

Maloney, William A. "Interest Groups and Social Capital." In *The Handbook of Social Capital*, edited by Dario Castiglione, Jan W. Van Deth and Guglielmo Wolleb. Oxford: Oxford University Press, 2008.

Mattingly, James E. "How to Become Your Own Worst Adversary: Examining the Connection Between Managerial Attributions and Organizational Relationships With Public Interest Stakeholders." *Journal of Public Affairs* 7 (2007): 7-21. Accessed through www.interscience.wiley.com (accessed on 9/1/11).

Maxwell, Kay J. "The League of Women Voters Through the Decades." Washington, DC: League of Women Voters booklet, 2007.

McCarthy, John D. "Persistence and Change Among Nationally-Federated Social Movements." In *Social Movements and Organization Theory*, edited by Gerald F. David et al. New York: Cambridge University Press, 2005.

McGerr, Michael. *A Fierce Discontent: The Rise and Fall of the Progressive Movement in America 1870 – 1920*. Oxford: Oxford University Press, 2003.

_____. "Political Style and Women's Power, 1830-1930." *The Journal of American History* 77, no. 3 (December 1990): 864-885.

McGrath, Michael. "Progressive Passion: Reviving the Fighting Spirit of Nonpartisan Reform." *National Civic Review* (Fall 2005): 20-28. http://www.interscience.wiley.com (accessed 10/14/10).

Ogden, David W. "League of Women Voters (LWV), Amicus Curiae." *Supreme Court Debates* 9, no. 4 (April 2006): 120-124. http://search.ebscohost.com/login.aspx?direct=true&db=aph&AN=20655846&site=ehost-live (accessed on 10/16/10).

Ogilvie, Robert S. *Voluntarism, Community Life, and the American Ethic.* Bloomington: Indiana University Press, 2004.

Olivier, Warner. "The League of Frightened Women." *Saturday Evening Post* 227, no. 17 (October 23, 1954): 32-102. http://search.ebscohost.com/login.aspx?direct=true&db=aph&AN=19452784&site=ehost-live (accessed on 9/16/10).

Olson, Mancur. *The Logic of Collective Action: Public Goods and the Theory of Groups.* Cambridge: Harvard University Press, 1971.

Palley, Marian Lief. "Beyond the Deadline." *PS* 15, no. 4 (Autumn 1982): 588-591. http://www.jstor.org/stable/419068 (accessed 10/28/10).

Pestritto, Ronald J. and William J. Atto. *American Progressivism: A Reader.* New York: Rowman and Littlefield Publishers, Inc., 2008.

Pierson, Paul, and Theda Skocpol. *The Transformation of American Politics: Activist Government and the Rise of Conservatism.* Princeton: Princeton University Press, 2007.

Popielarz, Pamela A., and J. Miller McPherson. "On the Edge or In Between: Niche Position, Niche Overlap, and the Duration of Voluntary Association Memberships." *The American Journal of Sociology* 101, no. 3 (November 1995): 698-720. http://www.jstor.org/stable/2781998 (accessed 2/3/11).

Putnam, Robert D. *Bowling Alone: The Collapse and Revival of American Community.* New York: Simon and Schuster, 2000.

_____. *Making Democracy Work: Civic Traditions in Modern Italy.* Princeton: Princeton University Press, 1993.

Rosenblum, Nancy. *Membership and Morals: The Personal Uses of Pluralism in America.* Princeton: Princeton University Press, 1998.

Sage Nonprofit Solutions. "Special Report: Legislation, Enforcement, Fraud, and Donor Skepticism." Austin: Sage Nonprofit Solutions, 2009.

Salisbury, Robert H. "An Exchange Theory of Groups." *Midwest Journal of Political Science* 13, no. 1 (February 1969): 1-32. http://www.jstor.org/stable/2110212 (accessed 2/2/11).

Sayre, Linda Damaris. "Volunteer Leaders: Learning and Development in the League of Women Voters." Ph.D. preview. New Brunswick: Rutgers The State University of New Jersey, 2002. http://0-proquest.umi.com.library.lausys.georgetown.edu/pqdweb?...t=PROD&VType=309&VName=PQD&TS=1287082428&clientld=5604 (accessed 10/14/10).

Schudson, Michael. *The Good Citizen: A History of American Civic Life.* Cambridge: Harvard University Press, 1999.

Schulte, Terriane K. "Citizen Experts: The League of Women Voters and Environmental Conservation." In "Special Issue on Women's Clubs," *Frontiers: A Journal of Women Studies* 30, no. 3 (2009): 1-29. http://search.ebscohost.com/login.aspx?direct=true&dbaph&AN=47903354&site=ehost-live (accessed 9/16/10).

Shklar, Judith N. *American Citizenship: The Quest for Inclusion.* Cambridge: Harvard University Press, 1991.

Skocpol, Theda. *Diminished Democracy: From Membership to Management in American Civic Life.* Norman: University of Oklahoma Press, 2003.

_____. "The Tocqueville Problem: Civic Engagement in American Democracy." *Social Science History* (Winter 1997): 455-479. http://www.jstor.org/stable/1171662 (accessed 11/19/10).

Skocpol, Theda, Marshall Ganz and Ziad Munson. "A Nation of Organizers: The Institutional Origins of Civic Voluntarism in the United States." *The American Political Science Review* 94, no. 3 (September

2000): 527-547. http://0-proquest.uni.com.library.lausys.georgetown. edu/pdqdlink?i...source=%24source&TS=1288188057&clientid=58117 &cc=1&TS=1288188057 (accessed 10/27/10).

Smith, Clagett G., and Arnold S. Tannenbaum. "Organizational Control Structure: A Comparative Analysis," *Human Relations* 16 (1963): 299-316. http://hum.sagepub.com/content/16/4/299.refs.html (accessed 10/28/10).

Stuhler, Barbara. *For the Public Record: A Documentary History of the League of Women Voters.* Westport: Greenwood Press, 2000.

Tannenbaum, Arnold S. "Control and Effectiveness in a Voluntary Organization." *The American Journal of Sociology* 67, no. 1 (July 1961): 33-46. http://www.jstor.org/stable/2772955 (accessed 10/28/10).

Threlkeld, Megan. "The Pan American Conference of Women, 1922: Successful Suffragists Turn to International Relations." *Diplomatic History* 31, no. 5 (November 2007): 801-828. http://search.ebscohost.com/login. aspx?direct=true&db=aph&AN=27476823&site=ehost-live (accessed 9/16/10).

Tocqueville, Alexis de. *Democracy in America.* Edited by J.P.Mayer, translated by George Lawrence. New York: Harper Perennial, 1969.

Verba, Sidney, Kay Lehman Schlozman, and Henry Brady. *Voice and Equality: Civic Voluntarism in American Politics.* Cambridge: Harvard University Press, 1995.

Vogel, David. "The Public Interest Movement and the American Reform Tradition." *Political Science Quarterly* 95, no. 4 (Winter 1980-1981): 607-627. http://www.jstor.org/stable/2150607 (accessed 10/14/10).

Warren, Mark E. *Democracy and Association.* Princeton: Princeton University Press, 2001.

_____, ed. *Democracy and Trust.* Cambridge: Cambridge University Press, 1999.

_____. "The Political Role of Non-profits in a Democracy," *Society* 4, no. 4 (May-June 2003): 46-51.

Watrous, Hilda R. "In League with Eleanor: Eleanor Roosevelt and the League of Women Voters, 1921-1962." New York: League of Women Voters of New York State booklet, 1984.

Wilenz, Sean. "Confounding Fathers." *The New Yorker* (October 18, 2010): 31-7.

Young, Louise. *In the Public Interest: The League of Women Voters 1920 – 1970 (Contributions in American Studies).* Westport: Greenwood Press, 1989.

Index

www.ingramcontent.com/pod-product-compliance
Lightning Source LLC
Chambersburg PA
CBHW020612270326
41927CB00005B/296